Learning to Type with BERNIE

JACK P. HOGGATT, ED.D.
Professor of Business Communication
University of Wisconsin — Eau Claire
Eau Claire, Wisconsin

THOMSON
SOUTH-WESTERN

Australia · Canada · Mexico · Singapore · Spain · United Kingdom · United States

THOMSON
SOUTH-WESTERN

Learning to Type with Bernie
Jack P. Hoggatt

VP/Editorial Director: Jack W. Calhoun

VP/Editor-in-Chief: Dave Shaut

Senior Publisher: Karen Schmohe

Acquisitions Editor: Jane Congdon

Project Manager: Dave Lafferty

Consulting Editor: Dianne Rankin

Production Manager: Patricia Matthews Boies

Production Editor: Colleen A. Farmer

VP/Director of Marketing: Carol Volz

Marketing Manager: Mike Cloran

Marketing Coordinator: Linda Kuper

Manufacturing Coordinator: Charlene Taylor

Design Project Manager: Stacy Jenkins Shirley

Compositor: Peter Lippincott

Cover/Internal Design: Grannan Graphic Design, Ltc.

Printer: Quebecor, Dubuque

Printed in the United States of America
1 2 3 4 5 07 06 05 04

ISBN: 0-538-43962-9

For more information contact South-Western, 5191 Natorp Boulevard, Mason, Ohio, 45040. Or you can visit our Internet site at: http://www.swlearning.com

More Learning Fun *with* BERNIE

Learning to Type is an Adventure, with Bernie's Typing Travels!

Learning has never been more fun than with Bernie's new-key learning software program for elementary students. Students help Bernie and Professor Keys recover lost experiment parts as they travel back in time, from Ancient Greece to the first moon landing.

Other features of Bernie's Typing Travels:

- Customizable *Spelling Experiments* provide typing practice and improve students' spelling skills.
- Built-in *Teacher Tool* helps you track progress, and complete *Teacher's Resource Guide* offers additional practice and teaching tips to help make keyboarding instruction easy.
- *Games* that students can play along the way help them practice keyboarding skills and offer motivation for improving skills.
- *Option to read and hear instructions in Spanish,* with actual lessons always presented in English, leaves no child behind in the learning process.

Students love being able to see their progress through performance graphs and achievement certificates.

Bernie's Typing Travels can be used in conjunction with other Bernie products, *Learning to Type with Bernie* and *Learning with Computers*!

www.bernielearning.com

Build a Strong Foundation for Keyboarding and Computer Applications Skills!

Bernie and friends guide students through *Learning with Computers,* a K-5 series of project-based books that introduce and reinforce important computer and core curriculum skills. Learning comes to life in this dynamic mix of all-around learning adventures and kid-focused fun that takes learning to the limits.

Levels K-2 focus on keyboarding and computer skills awareness, while *Levels 3-5* reinforce computer applications skills and help students gain proficiency in keyboarding, word processing, presentation, databases, spreadsheets, multimedia, and more!

Each project includes the following features:

- *Scenario* introduces the projects and puts learning in a real-life context.
- *Project Objectives* provide a clear blueprint of skills to be learned.
- *Word Power* familiarizes students with new computer terms.
- *Quick Checks* allow students to evaluate themselves and check their understanding.
- *On Your Own* offers opportunities for additional practice to reinforce skills learned.
- *Side Trips* are fun opportunities for additional cross-curricular activities that tie into core curriculum.
- *Typing Activity Page* teaches and builds keyboarding skills.

Experience the Best in Teacher Assistance!

Wrap Teacher's Edition contains reduced student pages and provides classroom-tested teaching suggestions, specific technology tips, and comprehensive guidance for success—even if you've never taught keyboarding and computer apps before!

Teacher's Resource CD provides everything necessary to complete the projects—data files, clip art, student and class rubrics, keyboarding methodology and technique sheets, letters to parents, and more!

Learning with Computers can be used independently or with *Bernie's Typing Travels* for a complete elementary computer curriculum.

Preface

Computers are used by most individuals on a daily basis in their personal and professional lives. Being able to operate a computer efficiently is rapidly becoming as important in the educational environment as it is in the business environment. As a result, many people believe that being able to operate a computer is as much a basic literacy skill as reading, writing, and arithmetic. One of the necessities for operating a computer efficiently is keyboarding skill.

Because computers are used to enhance the learning environment in most elementary schools, the need for elementary students to possess keyboarding skill is greater today than ever before. Having a computer that operates at the speed of light is of little value to individuals who can only operate it at the speed of a snail. Students who successfully complete the *Learning to Type with Bernie* book will be able to use the computer with greater proficiency.

Learning to Type with Bernie contains four units. Unit 1 teaches students to type by touch. Students must complete Unit 1 before going on to any of the other parts. Although students do not have to complete Unit 2 before completing Units 3 and 4, this plan is highly recommended. Unit 2 contains skill-building lessons designed to increase students' proficiency at the keyboard. After completing Unit 2, students will be much more comfortable at the keyboard, and the likelihood of their returning to the hunt-and-peck method of keying will be greatly diminished. Units 3 and 4 are included to give students a brief introduction to keying numbers and entering data via the numeric keypad.

Once you start using the book, Bernie (a mouse), Jake (a dog), and Professor Keys (a duck) will become members of your class. These characters are used in the book to keep the interest of young students while they learn to type by touch. A variety of activities with educational value beyond developing keyboarding skill are also included to maintain student interest. These activities include composing, spelling, vocabulary, geography, and history.

Teacher Support Materials

In addition to the student text, *Learning to Type with Bernie* comes with a four-color *Teacher's Manual*. The manual contains an overview of the text, objectives, lesson plans, teaching tips, ideas for games, tests, timing speed, charts, and articles on keyboarding instruction. The manual also includes references to the *Bernie's Typing Travels* software and the use of the *PowerPoint* presentations.

An Instructor's Resource CD is available for teachers who use *Learning to Type with Bernie*. This CD contains *PowerPoint* presentations, lesson plans, tests, timing speed charts, a keyboard chart, clip art, and other materials.

A set of adhesive stickers of the many characters in the text is available for creative uses by students and for use as incentives for students.

A wall chart set allows the classroom display of many key concepts for keyboarding and the use of computers.

Optional New-Key Learning Software Available

Optional for use with this text (as a separate purchase) is *Bernie's Typing Travels*, a new-key learning keyboarding software program with skill building appropriate for students in grades 3–5. This software includes numerous typing lessons, a graphics-packed word processor, printable certificates, editable spelling lists, a Teacher Tool, and a progress chart that shows how well students are doing. For more information, see www.berniestypingtravels.com. A separate three-ring bound *Teacher's Resource Guide* is also available for use with this software. The lessons in *Learning to Type with Bernie* can be used with any software, however.

About the Author

Dr. Jack P. Hoggatt is Department Chair for the Department of Business Communications at the University of Wisconsin-Eau Claire. A former advisor to local and state business organizations, Dr. Hoggatt is involved with his community and the school activities of his four children. He is an author of the best-selling *South-Western Century 21 Keyboarding and Computer Applications*, among other titles on keyboarding and the use of computers for all levels of instruction.

Dr. Hoggatt has worked with elementary keyboarding programs for more than 15 years. He has taught elementary students as well as presented methods courses on elementary keyboarding to elementary teachers and business education teachers.

Dedication

This book is dedicated to Glenda (my wife), Ashley, Logan, Erika, Cody (my children), and to Maxine Vermillion Hoggatt (my mother), who was a master teacher at providing the informal portion of my early education.

—*Jack Hoggatt*

Reviewers

The author gratefully thanks the following reviewers for their assistance in the development of this text.

Jan Anderson
Brookside Elementary School
Springville, UT

Dennis Batterman
Imperial Grade School
Imperial, NB

Karen Bean
Blinn Community College
Brenham, TX

Margaret Reed
Northside Elementary School
Hartford City, IN

Lori Sadler
Schnecksville Elementary School
Schnecksville, PA

Kathy Woodcock
Conway High School West
Conway, AR

Sue Zahnow
Prairie View Elementary School
East Troy, WI

How To Use This Book

Professor Keys provides helpful tips.

This line is for directions.

The keyboard shows the new keys being learned.

Bernie's Spelling Words helps spelling skills.

Sentences are the data to be keyed.

Drill lines are the data to be keyed.

Bernie also provides helpful tips.

GWAM indicates Gross Words a Minute.

Lesson 2

Reinforce Home Keys

Keep your fingers curved and upright.

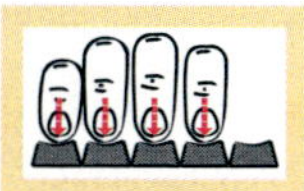

2a Practice Home Keys

Key each line once; double-space between 2-line groups.

1 f ff ff k kk kk s ss ss j
2 f ff ff k kk kk s ss ss j

3 a aa aa ; ;; ;; d dd dd l
4 a aa aa ; ;; ;; d dd dd l

5 jj ll kk ;; ss aa ff dd sk
6 jj ll kk ;; ss aa ff dd sk

7 ja dl s; fk lj sf af k;
8 ja dl s; fk lj sf af k;

Alphabetic Keys—**Lesson 2**

Skill Builder 1

Let's review the keys for letters A through I.

Bernie's Spelling Words

Key each word four times.

- very
- away
- show
- were
- park

1a Letter Review

Key each line twice; double-space between 2-line groups.

a 1 Anna Adams ate an apple and banana.
b 2 Bobby Cubbage bobbled the baseball.
c 3 Chuck checked on the cute raccoons.
d 4 Don decided to hide the old fiddle.
e 5 He believes it may rise three feet.
f 6 I shot fifty free throws on Friday.
g 7 Gregg, Glenda, and Gus were guests.
h 8 Here is the other half of the hymn.
i 9 I picked Illinois, Idaho, and Iowa.

GWAM 1' | 1 | 2 | 3 | 4 | 5 | 6 | 7 |

This text means that this is an easy exercise.

The dots and numbers above the words of the timing show the number of words per minute that you key.

Bernie's Vocabulary helps you learn new words.

Skill Builder 7

7d Timed Writings

Key two 1' timed writings on each paragraph. Determine your gwam on each timing.

Easy all letters used

How much time does it take you to return at the end of the line? Do you return with a lazy or a quick reach? Try not to stop at the end of the line; instead, return quickly and move down to the next line of copy.

How much time does it take you to strike the shift key and the letter to make a capital? Just a bit more practice will help you cut by half the time you are now using. When you cut the time, you increase your speed.

GWAM 1' | 1 | 2 | 3 | 4 | 5 | 6 | 7 | 8 | 9 | 10 |

Skill Builder 7

90

8 and 1

1b Famous Americans

Key the text below in paragraph form.

Crazy Horse

Famous people are quite often etched minds. Very famous people are etched in The images of just four of our presidents been carved in rock. They can be seen at Rushmore. A short distance from there is stone monument. It is also of a famous A who we will discuss next. His name is Crazy Horse.

Crazy Horse did all that he could to keep his land free. He did not want it taken over by settlers. Perhaps Crazy Horse is best known for the events at the Battle of the Little Bighorn. Crazy Horse and his men defeated Custer and his troops at this fight.

Bernie's Vocabulary

Do you know what these words mean?

- etched
- monument
- settlers

Number Keys—**Lesson 1**

100

Paragraphs are the exercises to be keyed.

To learn more about Learning to Type with Bernie, point your browser at www.typewithbernie.keyboarding.com and www.bernielearning.com

Contents

Unit 1

Alphabetic Keys

Objectives

In this unit you will learn to:

- Arrange your work area properly
- Sit correctly at a computer
- Type the alphabetic keys
- Type words and sentences
- Use correct keying techniques
- Think at the keyboard
- Compose at the keyboard

Lesson 1

Home Keys

I am Professor Loretta Keys. I will be your keyboarding instructor. Arrange your work area as shown at the right.

1a Learn Work Area Arrangement

Arrange your work area as shown below.

- Keyboard directly in front of chair; front edge of keyboard even with edge of desk
- Monitor placed for easy viewing
- Book at right of keyboard

4a Review Numeric Keypad (continued)

Drill 4

640	486	365	701	690	569
+150	+204	+495	+468	+254	+230
790	690	860	1,169	944	799

Drill 5

174	307	780	428	619	170
+589	+268	+196	+579	+357	+248
763	575	976	1,007	976	418

4b Keyboard Reinforcement

Key each line twice; double-space between 2-line groups.

h/s 1 She should shoot sixty shots a day.
i/r 2 Richard will write the eight firms.
j/q 3 Jacque J. Quin just quit the squad.
k/p 4 Kip keeps his backpack at the park.
l/o 5 Ron told Lola to look at the locks.
m/n 6 Minnie made many of the men a malt.

1b Learn Keying Position

Sit at the keyboard as instructed and shown below.

- Curve your fingers upright over the home keys.
- Keep your wrists low, but not touching the keyboard.
- Hold your forearms parallel to the slant of the keyboard.
- Keep your body erect, sitting back in the chair.
- Keep your feet on the floor.

Lesson 4

Review

Strike each key with a quick, sharp stroke using the tip of your finger.

Bernie's Spelling Words

Key each word four times.

- animals
- December
- different
- letter
- machine

4a Review Numeric Keypad

Use the calculator on your computer to do the drills below. Key the first number and strike the Plus (+) key. Key the second number and strike the Enter key. The number in blue is the answer.

Drill 1

130	248	460	185	249	357
+129	+576	+397	+352	+167	+864
259	824	857	537	416	1,221

Drill 2

809	903	214	768	350	119
+470	+66	+258	+595	+284	+730
1,279	969	472	1,363	634	849

Drill 3

312	406	879	102	398	475
+676	+859	+402	+219	+204	+657
988	1,265	1,281	321	602	1,132

Find the home keys on your keyboard (**a, s, d, f, j, k, l, ;**). Place your fingers on the home keys making sure to have them well curved and upright (not slanting).

1c Learn Home-Key Position

Home-key position for the left hand is **a, s, d, f**.

Home-key position for the right hand is **j, k, l, ;**.

1d Techniques: Keystroking and Space Bar

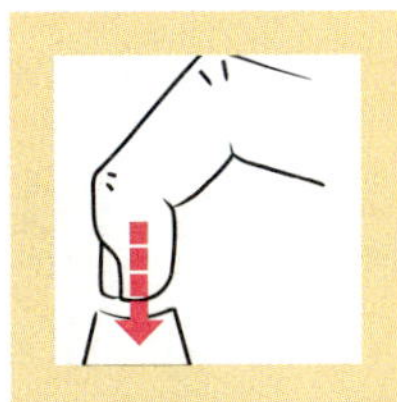

Keystroking: Strike each key with a light tap with the tip of the finger.

Spacing: Strike the **Space Bar** with the right thumb; use a quick down-and-in motion.

Bernie's Vocabulary

Do you know what these words mean?

- Hispanic
- humanitarian
- earthquake
- victims

3b Famous Americans

Key the text below in paragraph form.

Roberto Clemente

Baseball players who give a lot of help to their communities are recognized with the Roberto Clemente Award. Roberto Clemente was an excellent baseball player with the Pittsburgh Pirates. He was the complete player. He could hit. He could field. He could run, and he could throw.

Clemente was the first Hispanic player elected to the Baseball Hall of Fame. Not only was he quite the ballplayer, he was also a humanitarian. It was in this role that he lost his life. He was on a plane taking food and supplies to earthquake victims of Nicaragua. The plane crashed in the Caribbean Sea just after takeoff.

1e Practice Home Keys

- Place your fingers in home-key position. Key the line below.
- Strike the **Space Bar** after each letter you key.

f d s a j k l ; a s d f ; l k j

Use the **Enter** key to return the insertion point to the left of the screen and down one line.

1f Technique: Enter Key

1. Reach the little finger of the right hand to the **Enter** key. Tap the key and return the finger quickly to home-key position.
2. Key the line above two more times, using the **Enter** key to return at the end of the line each time.

Lesson 3

1, 2, and 3

- Use your index finger to strike the 1 key.
- Use your middle finger to strike the 2 key.
- Use your ring finger to strike the 3 key.

Bernie's Spelling Words

Key each word four times.

- afternoon
- August
- because
- brought
- laugh

3a Learn 1, 2, and 3

Use the calculator on your computer to do the drills below. Key the first number and strike the Plus (+) key. Key the second number and strike the Enter key. The number shown in blue is the answer.

Drill 1

1	2	3	1	2	1
+1	+2	+3	+3	+3	+2
2	4	6	4	5	3

Drill 2

12	13	31	32	21	33
+32	+22	+21	+12	+13	+11
44	35	52	44	34	44

Drill 3

102	328	520	173	281	390
+930	+516	+361	+429	+437	+612
1,032	844	881	602	718	1,002

1g Reinforce Home Keys

Key each line; double-space between 2-line groups.

Strike the **Enter** key twice to insert a double space between 2-line groups.

1 a aa aa l ll ll s ss ss ; ;; ;
2 a aa aa l ll ll s ss ss ; ;; ;

3 d dd dd j jj jj f ff ff k kk k
4 d dd dd j jj jj f ff ff k kk k

5 ss ff dd aa ll jj kk ;; ad sfs
6 ss ff dd aa ll jj kk ;; ad sfs

7 ll ff ss ;; dd jj aa kk kd asd
8 ll ff ss ;; dd jj aa kk kd asd

2a Learn 7, 8, and 9 (continued)

Drill 4

406	648	659	760	906	965
+750	+804	+954	+846	+754	+800
1,156	1,452	1,613	1,606	1,660	1,765

Drill 5

748	907	807	488	699	770
+598	+968	+796	+579	+857	+849
1,346	1,875	1,603	1,067	1,556	1,619

2b Keyboard Reinforcement

Key each line twice. Double-space between 2-line groups.

a/z 1 Zelda had a pizza party at the zoo.

b/y 2 The busy boy may buy Bobby a broom.

c/x 3 Six excited scouts can fix the box.

d/w 4 Wanda walked into those wild woods.

e/v 5 Evelyn gave Evan five heavy valves.

f/u 6 Only four of us found our uniforms.

g/t 7 Eight gifted girls bought the gift.

Lesson 2

Reinforce Home Keys

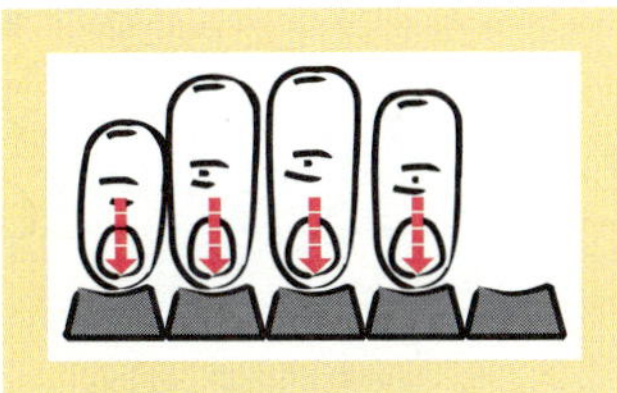

2a Practice Home Keys

Key each line once; double-space between 2-line groups.

1 f ff ff k kk kk s ss ss j jj j
2 f ff ff k kk kk s ss ss j jj j

3 a aa aa ; ;; ;; d dd dd l ll l
4 a aa aa ; ;; ;; d dd dd l ll l

5 jj ll kk ;; ss aa ff dd sk jkl
6 jj ll kk ;; ss aa ff dd sk jkl

7 ja dl s; fk lj sf af k; sfl
8 ja dl s; fk lj sf af k; sfl

Lesson 2

7, 8, and 9

- Use your index finger to strike the 7 key.
- Use your middle finger to strike the 8 key.
- Use your ring finger to strike the 9 key.

Bernie's Spelling Words

Key each word four times.

- computer
- next
- October
- people
- twenty

2a Learn 7, 8, and 9

Use the calculator on your computer to do the drills below. Key the first number and strike the* Plus *(+) key. Key the second number and strike the* Enter *key. The number shown in blue is the answer.

Drill 1

7	8	9	7	9	9
+7	+8	+9	+8	+7	+8
14	16	18	15	16	17

Drill 2

78	97	87	88	99	77
+98	+98	+79	+79	+87	+89
176	195	166	167	186	166

Drill 3

705	408	490	570	585	490
+960	+576	+765	+469	+467	+605
1,665	984	1,255	1,039	1,052	1,095

2b Technique: Enter Key

Key each line once; double-space between 2-line groups.

1 aa ss dd
2 aa ss dd

3 aa ss dd ff
4 aa ss dd ff

5 jj kk ll ;; ff
6 jj kk ll ;; ff

7 jj kk ll ;; ff dd
8 jj kk ll ;; ff dd

9 jj kk ll ;; ff dd ss
10 jj kk ll ;; ff dd ss

11 jj kk ll ;; ff dd ss aa
12 jj kk ll ;; ff dd ss aa

Bernie's Vocabulary

Do you know what these words mean?

- respect
- statesmen
- philosopher
- scientist
- diplomat

1b Famous Americans

Key the text below in paragraph form.

Benjamin Franklin

Respect the kid who brings your newspaper. He or she may be one of our next great leaders. One of the first jobs Benjamin Franklin had was that of delivering papers. Later in life he became recognized for the work he did in other areas.

He was a printer. He was an author. He was a philosopher. He is also known for his work as a scientist. In addition, he is quite well known for the work he did as a diplomat. He took part in the American Revolution. You combine all this, and you have one of the greatest statesmen of our country.

2c Key Words

Key each line once.

1 as as | ask ask | lad lad | dad dads
2 as as | ask ask | lad lad | dad dads

3 all all | sad sad | fall fall | add;
4 all all | sad sad | fall fall | add;

5 ad ad | as as; | lass lass | fad fad
6 ad ad | as as; | lass lass | fad fad

7 ask ask | adds adds | salad salad;
8 ask ask | adds adds | salad salad;

Lesson 1

4, 5, 6 and 0

Place your fingers on the numeric keypad with the

- index finger on 4
- middle finger on 5
- ring finger on 6
- thumb on 0

Bernie's Spelling Words

Key each word four times.

- disappoint
- March
- remember
- through
- while

1a Learn 4, 5, 6, and 0

Use the calculator on your computer to do the drills below. Key the first number and strike the Plus (+) key with your little finger. Key the second number and strike the Enter key. The number shown in blue is the answer.

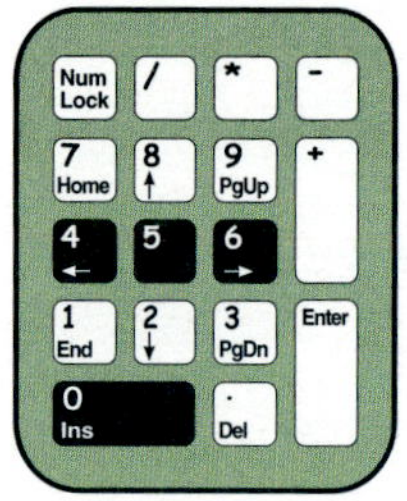

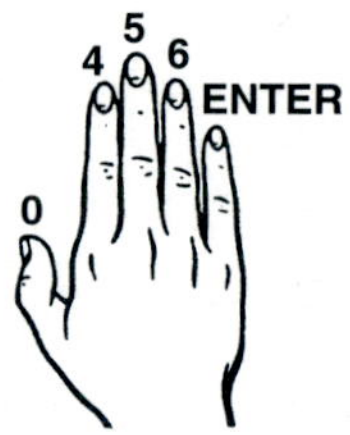

Drill 1

4	5	6	4	5	6
+4	+5	+6	+5	+6	+4
8	10	12	9	11	10

Drill 2

40	50	60	45	50	64
+50	+60	+40	+60	+54	+40
90	110	100	105	104	104

Drill 3

550	400	450	500	505	440
+406	+506	+465	+466	+460	+605
956	906	915	966	965	1,045

Lesson 3

e and n

3a Learn e and n

Key each line twice; double-space between 2-line groups.

Learn e

1 d e d e de de ed ed deed deed;
2 elk feel seek lake jade; lead;
3 sale desk feed safe flake jell

Learn n

4 j n j n jn jn nj nj an and and
5 an fan fan | and; and; | lank lank
6 sand sand | land land | sank sank;

Practice e and n

7 need den false lane sane desk;
8 end knees send ankle fan seek;
9 fed and sea fan need land lake

Unit 4 Numeric Keypad

Objectives

In this unit you will:

- Learn the numeric keypad
- Type sentences and paragraphs
- Use correct keying techniques
- Learn to spell words
- Learn new vocabulary words

3b Reinforce e and n

Key each line twice; double-space between 2-line groups.

Key letters

1 ae se de fe je ke le ;e es ej;
2 na ns nd nf nj nk nl n; ne kn;
3 ne nje ekn nae dne nel n;e sne

Key words

4 less less | deaf deaf | feed feed;
5 fan fan; | sank sank | land; land;
6 den den | need need | jeans jeans;

Key phrases

7 need a fan | send a | seek an end;
8 and a | need a desk | land and sea
9 and less | see a sad lad | ask dad

Don't stop or pause between words.

6b Number Reinforcement

Key each line. Tab between columns so all of the items in the column line up. You will have to tab a different number of times in each line, depending on the number of spaces in the state name.

First Ten States

	State		Date
1	Delaware	tab →	December 7, 1787
2	Pennsylvania	tab →	December 12, 1787
3	New Jersey	tab →	December 18, 1787
4	Georgia	tab →	January 2, 1788
5	Connecticut	tab →	January 9, 1788
6	Massachusetts	tab →	February 6, 1788
7	Maryland	tab →	April 28, 1788
8	South Carolina	tab →	May 23, 1788
9	New Hampshire	tab →	June 21, 1788
10	Virginia	tab →	June 25, 1788

3c Speed Building

Key each line once; double-space between 2-line groups.

1 elf elf and and sled sled lake

2 jade fled sand sled asked fall

3 sea add leek desk salad sales;

4 a sad dad; all fall ads; jeans

5 feed a lad; desks and fans; ask a;

6 all lakes; jade desk; a lass fell

Don't rest your palms on the keyboard or desk as you key.

Lesson 6

Review

Bernie's Spelling Words

Key each word four times.

- April
- birthday
- flower
- measure
- mouth

6a Numbers Review

Key each line twice; double-space between 2-line groups.

1 Miguel paid for 29 of the 94 meals.
2 Deliver a paper to 3876 Cedar Lane.
3 Their score was 14 to 5 on June 20.
4 The play will be on June 14 and 25.
5 Javier Lopez hit 43 homers in 2003.
6 M. Prior won 18 and lost 6 in 2003.
7 Jon keyed 56 wpm; Jan keyed 57 wpm.
8 Robert Chen bowled 96, 87, and 118.
9 Jane sold 79 red and 97 pink roses.

GWAM 1' | 1 | 2 | 3 | 4 | 5 | 6 | 7 |

Lesson 4

Review

Meet Jake; he is our techniques officer. If you do what he says, your skill will improve.

4a Home Keys

Key each line once; double-space between 2-line groups.

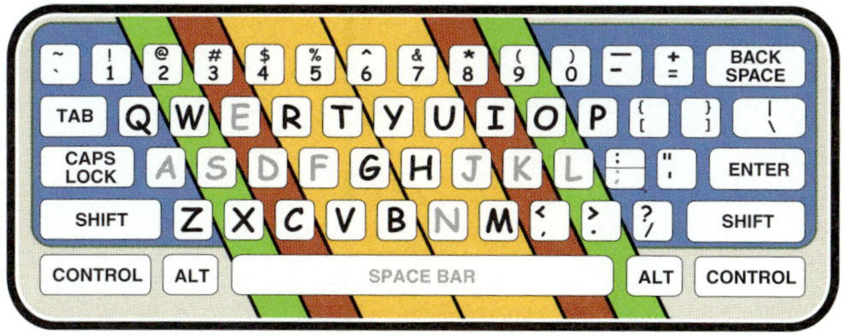

1 aa kk ff ss jj ;; dd ll kk jj;
2 aa kk ff ss jj ;; dd ll kk jj;

3 js kf ld ;a dj f; sk al kj ds;
4 js kf ld ;a dj f; sk al kj ds;

5 sad sad | fad fad | lad lad | as as;
6 sad sad | fad fad | lad lad | as as;

7 all fall; all fall | ask dad; ask dad
8 all fall; all fall | ask dad; ask dad

6 and 2

Bernie's Vocabulary

Do you know what these words mean?

- ultimate
- excellent
- recognized

5b Famous Americans

Key the text below in paragraph form.

Babe Ruth

Most kids have dreams. Many dream of being a sports hero. Some dream of scoring a touchdown to win the game. Others dream of sinking a basket to win the game. To others, however, the ultimate is hitting the home run that wins the game. Babe Ruth was able quite often to live the dream of many kids. He hit just over seven hundred home runs.

Ruth is remembered for the home runs he hit. But he was also an excellent pitcher. He won twice as many games as he lost. Ruth played his last game about seventy years ago. But he is still recognized as one of the greatest players to ever play the game.

4b All Keys Learned

Key each line once; double-space between 2-line groups.

1 ee le fe ;e ke de je se ae e;n
2 ee le fe ;e ke de je se ae e;n

3 nn nd na nj ns n; nk nf nl n;n
4 nn nd na nj ns n; nk nf nl n;n

5 lake lake | jeans jeans | fed fed
6 lake lake | jeans jeans | fed fed

7 a jade sale; a desk fan; a lad
8 as a; dad feels sad; a fall ad

Lesson 5

6 and 2

After you finish this lesson, you will know how to key all of the numbers on the top row.

Bernie's Spelling Words

Key each word four times.

- always
- November
- number
- Thursday
- yellow

5a Learn 6 and 2

Key each line twice; double-space between 2-line groups.

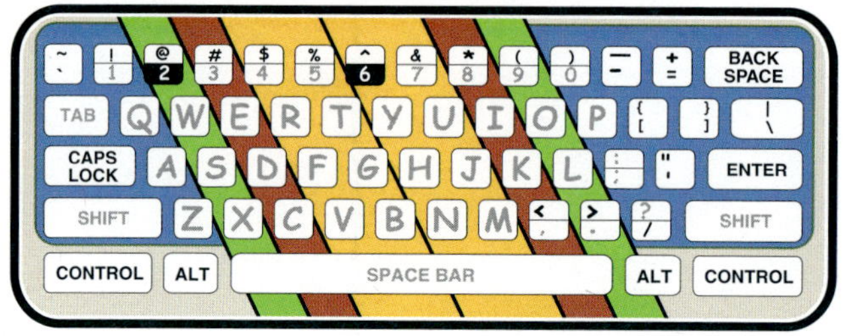

Learn 6

1. j 6 j 6 j6j 6j6 66 j6j6 6j6j 6
2. ab6 cd6 ef6 gh6 ij6 kl6 mn6 o6
3. 6pq 6rs 6tu 6vw 6xy 6z6 y6y 66

Learn 2

4. s 2 s 2 s2s 2s2 22 s2s2 2s2s 2
5. a2b c2d e2f g2h i2j k2l m2n 2o
6. 2p2 q2r 2s2 t2u 2v2 w2x 2y2 z2

Practice numbers

7. Juan Vasquez hit .326 in 2003.
8. I played 18 holes on April 19.
9. Luke paid 47 cents; I paid 53.

4c Technique: Enter Key

Key each line twice. At the end of each line, strike the Enter key and immediately begin keying the next line.

1. an
2. den
3. ankle
4. and flakes
5. land and sea
6. need a desk fan
7. a lass needs a desk
8. land; sand; sea; lake;

4d Something Extra

Unscramble the letters below to create ten words. Key those words.

nde	nfa	dna	lek	eas
lnda	edne	dkes	aelk	aedj

7 and 3

Don't look at the keyboard when you key numbers.

4b Reinforce Numbers

Key the text below in paragraph form.

George Washington was our first President. He was from Virginia. He took office in 1789. He stayed in that office until 1797. John Adams was our second President. He was born on the 30th of October in the year 1735. He took office in 1797. He held the office for four years. Adams was from the state of Massachusetts.

Our third President was Thomas Jefferson. He was born on the 13th of April. The year he was born was 1743. He was the second President to come from the state of Virginia. He served as our leader until the year 1809. Before he became President, he helped draft the Declaration of Independence. It was during his term in office that the Louisiana Territory was bought. The price paid for this land was 15 million dollars.

Lesson 5

o and t

Keep your fingers curved and upright.

5a Learn o and t

Key each line twice; double-space between 2-line groups.

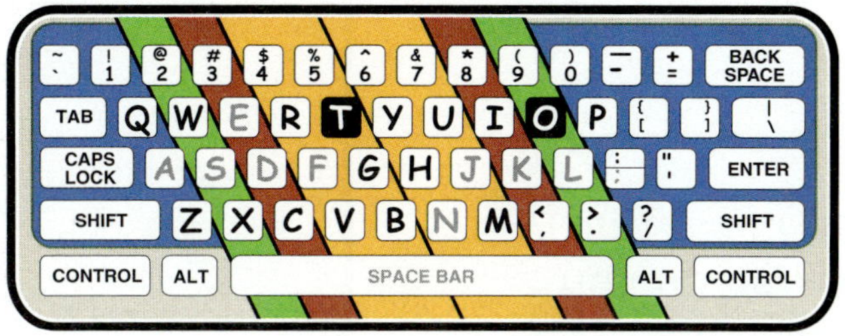

Learn o

1 l o l o lo lo olo olo old old;
2 noon noon | sold sold | doll doll;
3 joke does lone fold soak loads

Learn t

4 f t f t ft ft tf tf tend tend;
5 at at | sat sat; | eat eat | jet jet
6 late date take last talk feast

Practice o and t

7 ton oat jot lot foot toes told
8 took told done jolt salt toads
9 oak jets toll soft float total

Lesson 4

7 and 3

Numbers are important! How many ways can you think to use numbers?

Bernie's Spelling Words

Key each word four times.

- February
- quick
- receive
- until
- voice

4a Learn 7 and 3

Key each line twice; double-space between 2-line groups.

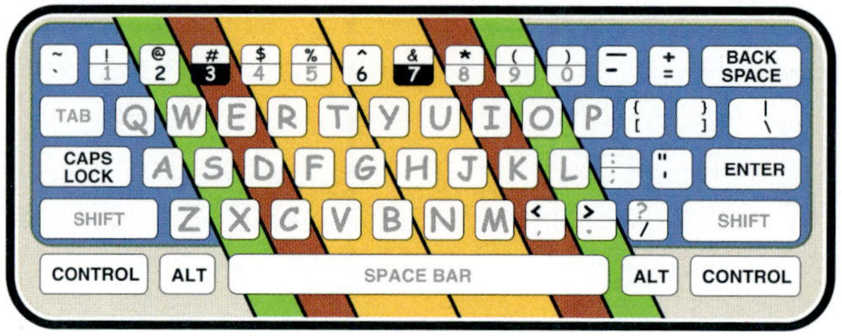

Learn 7

1. j 7 j 7 j7j 7j7 77 j7j7 7j7j 7
2. z7y x7w v7u t7s r7q p7o n7m l7
3. k7j 7i7 h7g 7f7 e7d 7c7 b7a 77

Learn 3

4. d 3 d 3 d3d 3d3 33 d3d3 3d3d 3
5. q3q 3c3 w3w 3j3 z3z 3k3 x3x f3
6. b3b 3h3 m3m 3g3 v3v 3n3 p3p u3

Practice numbers

7. Kate wanted number 13, not 17.
8. The combination was 50.49.387.
9. They said June 17 and June 18.

5b Reinforce o and t

Key each line twice; double-space between 2-line groups.

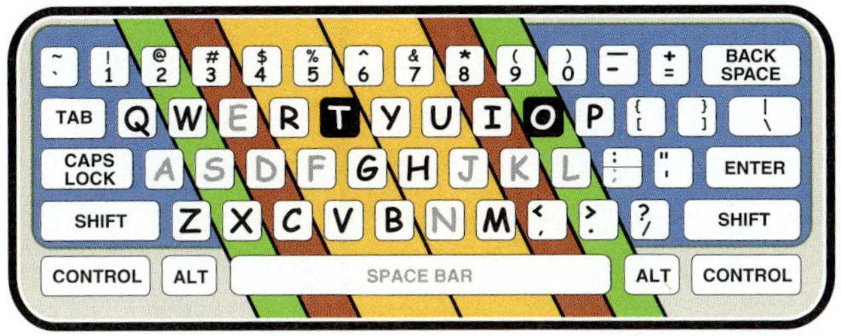

Key letters

1 so ;o fo lo do jo ao ko no eo;

2 tj td tl ta t; ts tk tf te nt;

3 ot tfo okt tao dto otl o;t sto

Key words

4 loan loan | does does | look look;

5 ten ten; | tank tank | jets; jets;

6 not not | dots dots | tones tones;

Key phrases

7 a lake lot | not as | took a look;

8 a ton | needs a tent | not as late

9 too late | sent a note | odd lots;

Bernie's Vocabulary

Do you know what these words mean?

- freedom
- admirable
- slave
- escape
- spy

3b Famous Americans

Key the text below in paragraph form.

Harriet Tubman

Risking your own life for the freedom of others has always been viewed as an admirable thing to do. Harriet Tubman was a slave in the South. She became a free woman when she escaped to the North. This freedom just did not mean much to her while so many others were still slaves.

She quickly risked her own life by going back into the South. She did this to help other slaves escape. She was able to help several hundred. This is an amazingly large number. During the Civil War she continued to exhibit the traits of a hero. She served the Union as a spy and as a scout.

Remember, don't look at the keys as you key the words!

jet	odd
late	ten
loan	tent
noon	ton
old	soft

5c Space Bar Technique

Key each line twice; double-space between 2-line groups. Strike the Space Bar immediately after keying each word.

1 do do | of of | no no | to to | so so;
2 jet jet | ask ask | old old | no no;
3 knee knee | sand sand | need need;

5d Thinking at the Keyboard

Read the sentences below. From the list at the left, choose the word that best completes the sentence. Key the word and strike the Enter key.

1 The opposite of young is ________.
2 You go to the bank to get a ________.
3 You may sleep in a ________ when you camp.
4 The opposite of hard is ________.
5 Another name for 12 o'clock is ________.
6 5 + 5 = ________.
7 The opposite of early is ________.
8 Numbers 1, 3, and 5 are ________ numbers.
9 A type of airplane is a ________.
10 Two thousand pounds equals a ________.

Lesson 3

0 and 5

Bernie's Spelling Words

Key each word four times.

- doctor
- school
- September
- should
- Tuesday

3a Learn 0 and 5

Key each line twice; double-space between 2-line groups.

Learn 0

1 ; 0 ; 0 ;0; 0;0 00 ;0;0 0;0; 0

2 a0b c0d e0f g0h i0j k0l m0n p0

3 p0q r0s t0u v0w x0y z0z 0z0 00

Learn 5

4 f 5 f 5 f5f 5f5 55 f5f5 5f5f 5

5 x5x 5d5 y5y 5j5 q5q 5k5 c5c e5

6 z5z 5h5 m5m 5g5 n5n 5e5 p5p u5

Practice numbers

7 Jan added 5 and 10 and got 15.

8 Nick was born in 1949 or 1950.

9 Is my locker 508, 509, or 510?

Lesson 6

i and r

6a Learn i and r

Key each line twice; double-space between 2-line groups.

Learn i

1 k i k i ki ki ik ik kids kids;

2 like like | fine fine | jail jail;

3 it is ill nail join fine jail;

Learn r

4 f r f r fr fr rf rf fort fort;

5 rat rat; | are are | errand errand

6 rod jar error tear rake learn;

Practice i and r

7 kind raft sink road knit soar;

8 fair iron rink risk; irritate;

9 fire tire ride liar rind rider

9 and 4

2b Reinforce Numbers

Key the text below in paragraph form.

Interesting State Facts

In 1818 Illinois became a state. Springfield is the capital of the state. Alabama was the next to become a state. That took place on the 18th of December in the year 1889. The capital of Alabama is Montgomery.

There were four more states that joined the Union in 1889. The first states to join were North and South Dakota. Montana was the next state to join that year. It became a state on November 8. Montana was the 41st state. Washington was the last to join that year. It became a state three days later on the 11th.

6b Reinforce i and r

Key each line twice; double-space between 2-line groups.

Key letters

1. ki oi ti ei ni ji fi di ki li;
2. fr sr jr ar kr sr ro re rn rt;
3. ir ilr ijr itr rni roi rei rki

Key words

4. kind kind | like like | dine dine;
5. are are; | rate rate | jars; jars;
6. liar liar | rink rink | tire tire;

Key phrases

7. not an iron | risk a lot | on fire
8. are real | to irritate | did rinse
9. did a refill | looks like a riot

Lesson 2

9 and 4

Reach to the number keys with your fingers. Do not move your entire hand up to the number row.

Bernie's Spelling Words

Key each word four times.

- change
- Internet
- judge
- sister
- street

2a Learn 9 and 4

Key each line twice; double-space between 2-line groups.

Learn 9

1 l 9 l 9 l9l 9l9 99 l9l9 9l9l 9

2 9ab c9d ef9 9gh i9j kl9 9mn o9

3 9pq r9s tu9 9vw x9y zz9 9qx c9

Learn 4

4 f 4 f 4 f4f 4f4 44 f4f4 4f4f 4

5 ab4 c4d 4ef gh4 i4j 4kl 4mn o4

6 qp4 r4s 4tu vw4 x4y jk4 m4n p4

Practice numbers

7 Of 498 students, 194 got an A.

8 Jay added 9, 4, 8, 1, 9, and 4.

9 Felipe bowled 94, 119, and 84.

6c Speed Building

The sentences below contain balanced-hand words. Key each line twice; double-space between 2-line groups.

1 air did end for or rid sir aid

2 do laid oak risk so to an iris

3 sod if also lend is of sit doe

4 lake take and dial it ant torn

5 land rifle title flake orient;

6 field fork lane odor idle foal

Quickly space after each word and immediately begin keying the next word.

1b Famous Americans

Key the text below in paragraph form.

Crazy Horse

Famous people are quite often etched in our minds. Very famous people are etched in stone. The images of just four of our presidents have been carved in rock. They can be seen at Mt. Rushmore. A short distance from there is another stone monument. It is also of a famous American who we will discuss next. His name is Crazy Horse.

Crazy Horse did all that he could to keep his land free. He did not want it taken over by settlers. Perhaps Crazy Horse is best known for the events at the Battle of the Little Bighorn. Crazy Horse and his men defeated Custer and his troops at this fight.

Bernie's Vocabulary

Do you know what these words mean?

- etched
- monument
- settlers

Lesson 7

Review

7a Short, Easy Words

Key each line once; double-space between 2-line groups.

1 an an | if if | as as | to to | no no;
2 an an | if if | as as | to to | no no;

3 ten ten | are are | jar jar | do do;
4 ten ten | are are | jar jar | do do;

5 ask ask | off off | old old | on on;
6 ask ask | off off | old old | on on;

7 tire tire | joke joke | soak soak;
8 tire tire | joke joke | soak soak;

Lesson 1

8 and 1

The reaches to the numbers will be easier if you keep your fingers curved. Don't rest the palms of your hands on the keyboard.

Bernie's Spelling Words

Key each word four times.

- definite
- occur
- separate
- Wednesday
- yield

1a Learn 8 and 1

Key each line twice; double-space between 2-line groups.

Learn 8

1. k 8 k 8 k8k 8k8 88 k8k8 8k8k 8
2. a8b c8d e8f g8h i8j k8l m8n o8
3. 8p8 q8r 8s8 t8u 8v8 w8x 8y8 z8

Learn 1

4. a 1 a 1 a1a 1a1 11 a1a1 1a1a 1
5. a1b c1d e1f g1h i1j k1l m1n o1
6. 1p1 q1r 1s1 t1u 1v1 w1x 1y1 z1

Practice numbers

7. Only 118 of 818 boys finished.
8. He sent 18 letters on June 18.
9. Maria had scores of 81 and 88.

7b Short-word Phrases

Key each line once; double-space between 2-line groups.

1 is a | and if | are not | look at it
2 is a | and if | are not | look at it

3 did not | as if | read it | fast jet
4 did not | as if | read it | fast jet

5 ask a dad | roll off | an old tire
6 ask a dad | roll off | an old tire

7 joke a lot | at a lake | sales ad;
8 joke a lot | at a lake | sales ad;

Unit 3

Number Keys

Objectives

In this unit you will:

- Learn the number keys
- Type words, sentences, and paragraphs
- Use correct keying techniques
- Learn to spell words
- Learn new vocabulary words
- Learn about famous Americans

Press **Enter** quickly at the end of the line and immediately begin the next line.

Can you unscramble these letters to make words?

7c Technique: Enter Key

Key each line twice. At the end of each line, strike the Enter key and immediately begin keying the next line.

1. and
2. a red
3. all ads
4. flat tire
5. near a kid
6. like an aide
7. a fast red jet
8. kid needs a sled

7d Something Extra

Unscramble the letters below to create ten words. Key those words.

rja	dol	aks	nto	tol
atsf	ejko	kosa	rdea	oklo

Bernie's Vocabulary

Do you know what these words or terms mean?

- fortunate
- United Nations
- promote

10b Famous Americans

Key the text below in paragraph form.

Eleanor Roosevelt

You must be a very special person if you are recognized all over the world. Eleanor Roosevelt was such a person. All through her life, she took up the cause of the less fortunate. Quite often you could find her trying to help people or fix problems.

She worked on women's issues. She worked on racial issues. She worked on youth issues. She spent a lot of time working on these causes. As the first lady, she was able to further these causes. Serving on the United Nations gave her the opportunity to continue to promote these just causes on the world level.

Lesson 8

h and left shift

Learn to Key Capital Letters

Use these three steps to key capital letters with the right hand:

1. Hold down the **Left Shift** key with the little finger on the left hand.
2. Strike the letter with the right hand.
3. Return finger(s) to home keys.

8a Learn h and left shift

Key each line twice; double-space between 2-line groups.

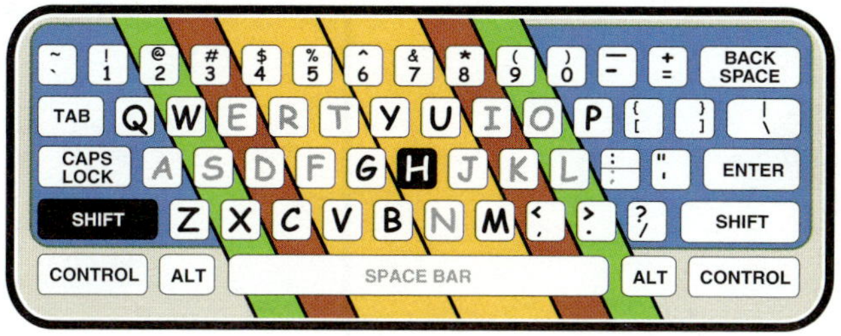

Learn h

1 j h j h jh jh hj hj half half;
2 he he | had had | hit hit | hoe hoe;
3 the hike half north shade she;

Learn left shift

4 a J a J a K a K a L a L a O a;
5 Jake Jake | Kent Kent | Neal Neal;
6 Jane Ishii; Jake Haas; Ken Lee

Practice h and left shift

7 Oak Lake Lane; Hans had a hit;
8 hold their then hero dash than
9 Idaho; Jo; Ohio; Hank; Kansas;

Skill Builder 10

Bernie's Spelling Words

Key each word four times.

- before
- college
- found
- piece
- think

10a Balanced-hand Sentences

Key each sentence twice. Try to key faster the second time you key the line.

1. Their firm paid Kent for the signs.
2. Jay did all of the map work for us.
3. Kent may make all the forms for us.
4. Jana may do the audit for the firm.
5. Did Helen lend the firms the forms?
6. Dick may hang the sign on the door.
7. Jane paid the man for the six keys.
8. If she pays for the bus, he may go.

GWAM 1' | 1 | 2 | 3 | 4 | 5 | 6 | 7 |

8b Reinforce h and left shift

Key each line twice; double-space between 2-line groups.

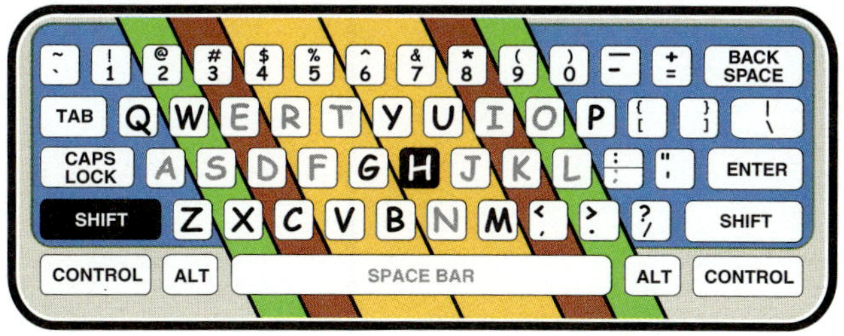

Key letters

1. ih rh nh jh th eh oh lh kh dh;
2. rJ iK dN aL fO sI JoI NeL Krt;
3. Jh Kih Nih Ith Onh Loh Hre Jth

Key words

4. Hans Hans | Josh Josh | then then;
5. Nate Nate | hold hold | Hank Hank;
6. Kate Kate | has has | Haiti Haiti;

Key phrases

7. Jake had a | red hair | three hits
8. Ida has half | a hit | has a horse
9. Janet has those; | here or there

9d Timed Writings

Key two 1' timed writings on each paragraph. Determine your gwam on each timing.

You should have increased your typing speed since your last timed writings. Let's see.

Easy all letters used

Time and motion are essential elements for increasing your keying speed. As you make each move to key a letter, you use time. So you want to be sure that every move is quick and direct. You can cut time and increase speed in this way.

A good way to reduce motion and thus save time is to make the fingers stay in home position as the reach to each letter is made. Keep your gaze on the copy. Then, just reach to the next key. Use a low, direct reach at your best rate of speed.

GWAM 1' | 1 | 2 | 3 | 4 | 5 | 6 | 7 | 8 | 9 | 10 |

8c Space Bar Technique

Key each line twice; double-space between 2-line groups. Strike the Space Bar immediately after keying each word and immediately begin the next word.

1 see see | off off | ill ill | to to;
2 odd odd | tee tee | all all | no no;
3 hill hill | Jeff Jeff | Jill Jill;

8d Thinking at the Keyboard

Read the sentences below. From the list at the left, choose the word that best completes the sentence. Key the word and strike the Enter key.

half	raft
horse	sale
Idaho	tires
kind	their
north	there

1. Cars have four ________.
2. The opposite of mean is ________.
3. You can float on water with a ________.
4. You get a special deal on ________ items.
5. Cut the cake in ________.
6. The opposite of south is ________.
7. The state known for potatoes is ________.
8. People often confuse there and ________.
9. You ride a ________.
10. By adding a **t** to here you have ________.

9b Speed Check

Key two 20-second (20") timed writings on each line. Key the line as many times as you can in 20".

1. I bought a car.
2. Maria was very late.
3. Vanessa was quite amazed.
4. The exam took over four hours.
5. Jon placed third in the final race.

20" | 3 | 6 | 9 | 12 | 15 | 18 | 21

9c Where is Bernie?

Key each line twice. As you key the lines, figure out which city Bernie is visiting. Key the name of the city at the end of line 6.

1. The Alamo is a famous landmark of this city.
2. This city is located in the state of Texas.
3. David Crockett and James Bowie died here.
4. Sam Houston fought to recapture this city.
5. This city has a River Walk downtown.
6. The name of the city is ___________.

Where is Bernie?

Lesson 9

c and y

9a Learn c and y

Key each line twice; double-space between 2-line groups.

Learn c

1 d c d c dc dc cd cd code code;
2 card card | cone cone | cent cent;
3 Jack race tack sick coat chase

Learn y

4 j y j y jy jy yj yjy Jay; Jay;
5 yard yard | hay hay | today today;
6 yet day say hay yes yarn Jayne

Practice c and y

7 fancy classy tacky ratty Nancy
8 fly only sack richly accident;
9 clay yield ached Cary and Cody

Skill Builder 9

Bernie's Spelling Words

Key each word four times.

- June
- music
- noise
- thumb
- zebra

9a Skill Building

Key each sentence twice. Try to key faster the second time you key the line.

Balanced-hand words

1 box due dog own may sit cow six for
2 half dish held kept rich name shelf

3 The city may pay both of the girls.
4 Jan owns the auto down by the dock.
5 Their goal is to pay the eight men.

One-hand words

6 dad bat art you joy oil fee hop sea
7 face look fade only safe pink extra

8 Johnny read Fred my best tax cases.
9 Get a tax card after we set a date.
10 You are free to act on my tax case.

GWAM 1' | 1 | 2 | 3 | 4 | 5 | 6 | 7 |

Key the word faster the second time you key it in lines 4-6.

9b Reinforce c and y

Key each line twice; double-space between 2-line groups.

Key letters

1 hc ry nc jy tc ey oc ly kc dy;
2 rc iy dc aY fc sy jc yc yi cnc
3 Jy Lca Iys Ncr Hyd Kce Oyf Yc;

Key words

4 yet yet | cocoa cocoa | eyes eyes;
5 cyst cyst | cycle cycle | yes yes;
6 clay clay | toy toy | candy candy;

Key phrases

7 the cake | not yet | they can yell
8 the candle | yield the | Nancy can
9 Lacy cycled | cry for a | lick the

Bernie's Vocabulary

Do you know what these words or terms mean?

- Civil War
- recognized
- schooling

8b Famous Americans

Key the text below in paragraph form.

Abraham Lincoln

His mother signed her name with an X. His father had no schooling. Could a President come from such a background? President Lincoln did. Lincoln was not just a President. He is quite often recognized as one of the best presidents to ever hold the office.

Lincoln was often called Honest Abe. He always gave the extra effort. Because of this, he was a success. Whether the job was splitting logs, being a lawyer, or being President, he gave it his best. Dealing with the Civil War required a man who gave his best.

c and y

9c Speed Building

Key each line twice; double-space between 2-line groups.

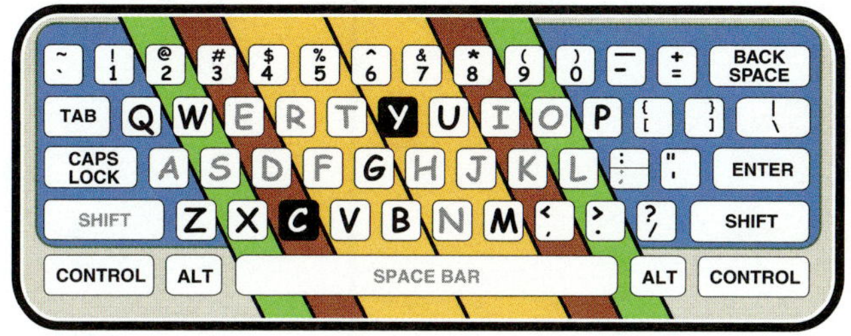

1 half dock end keys she the city

2 lay sick hand did rye and clay

3 they coal do for held then cot

4 hair shanty social corn handle

5 chair shelf their shake theory

6 Hal Kris Jay Jane Keith Nancy;

Skill Builder 8

Bernie's Spelling Words

Key each word four times.

- earth
- eight
- money
- small
- whole

8a Balanced-hand Sentences

Key each sentence twice. Try to key faster the second time you key the line.

1 Heidi may go to the social with us.

2 I may go to the city to visit Todd.

3 Kris is too busy to go to the lake.

4 Helen may sign all the audit forms.

5 The maid is to rush the bowl to us.

6 Rob and Jane saw an antique mantle.

7 Sidney kept the emblems in the box.

8 Kent kept half of their hay for us.

GWAM 1' | 1 | 2 | 3 | 4 | 5 | 6 | 7 |

Lesson 10

Review

10a Short, Easy Words

Key each line once; double-space between 2-line groups.

1 and and | ask ask | jet jet | an an;
2 and and | ask ask | jet jet | an an;

3 talk talk | fire fire | hold hold;
4 talk talk | fire fire | hold hold;

5 Jack Jack | yield yield | fed fed;
6 Jack Jack | yield yield | fed fed;

7 jello jello | fork fork | ice ice;
8 jello jello | fork fork | ice ice;

7d Timed Writings

Key two 1' timed writings on each paragraph. Determine your gwam on each timing.

Easy all letters used

How much time does it take you to return at the end of the line? Do you return with a lazy or a quick reach? Try not to stop at the end of the line; instead, return quickly and move down to the next line of copy.

How much time does it take you to strike the shift key and the letter to make a capital? Just a bit more practice will help you cut by half the time you are now using. When you cut the time, you increase your speed.

GWAM 1' | 1 | 2 | 3 | 4 | 5 | 6 | 7 | 8 | 9 | 10 |

Remember to keep your eyes on the copy as you key.

10b Short, Easy Phrases

Key each line once; double-space between 2-line groups.

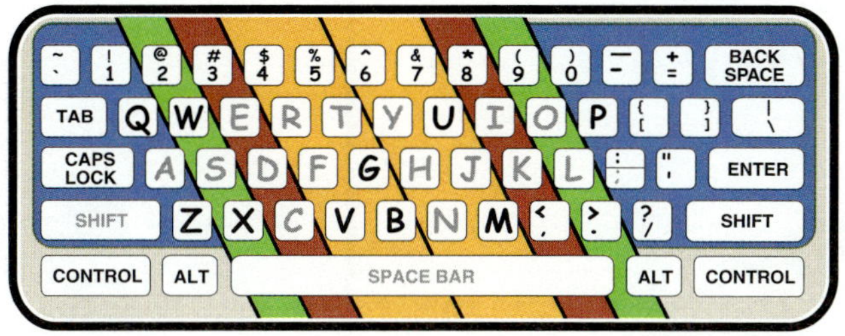

1 if she | did he | had the | she left
2 if she | did he | had the | she left

3 a joke | ask for | old list | to the
4 a joke | ask for | old list | to the

5 did not send | yes or no | to Cody
6 did not send | yes or no | to Cody

7 Kent said | for the lark | Jane is
8 Kent said | for the lark | Jane is

7b Speed Check

Key two 20-second (20") timed writings on each line. Key the line as many times as you can in 20".

3 | 6 | 9 | 12 | 15 | 18 | 21

1. I saw the game.
2. Jen was in the play.
3. When did you buy the car?
4. Mr. Valdez kept the playbook.
5. Jane did not quite finish the exam.

20" | 3 | 6 | 9 | 12 | 15 | 18 | 21 |

Where is Bernie?

7c Where is Bernie?

Key each line twice. As you key the lines, figure out which city Bernie is visiting. Key the name of the city at the end of line 6.

1. This city is located along the Potomac River.
2. You can visit the White House in this city.
3. The Lincoln Memorial can be seen here.
4. You can go to the Smithsonian Institute here.
5. The city is the capital of the U.S.A.
6. The name of the city is ____________.

10c Technique: Enter Key

Key each line twice. At the end of each line, strike the Enter key and immediately begin keying the next line.

1. Ken left
2. on a train
3. for the disk
4. is to take all
5. Jan said he left
6. yield for the cars
7. call if I can take a
8. as soon as she needs a

10d Something Extra

Unscramble the letters below to create ten words. Key those words.

ylac	odlt	dkes	teno	nsde
seey	iytc	reca	ncio	jnoi

Skill Builder 7

If you are putting in the effort, your speed should be higher.

Bernie's Spelling Words

Key each word four times.

- first
- July
- quit
- sound
- Sunday

7a Balanced-hand Sentences

Key each sentence twice. Try to key faster the second time you key the line.

1. Jake may sign all the forms for us.
2. Helen may do the work for the maid.
3. Pamela may pay the man for the bus.
4. He did make a right turn by a sign.
5. Orlando paid the maid for the work.
6. Jay and Kay own both of the chairs.
7. When did the auditor sign the form?
8. Vivian paid the man to fix the bus.

GWAM 1' | 1 | 2 | 3 | 4 | 5 | 6 | 7 |

Lesson 11

period (.) and u

Space **twice** after a period (.) at the end of a sentence except at line endings. There, press **Enter** without spacing.

11a Learn period (.) and u

Key each line twice; double-space between 2-line groups.

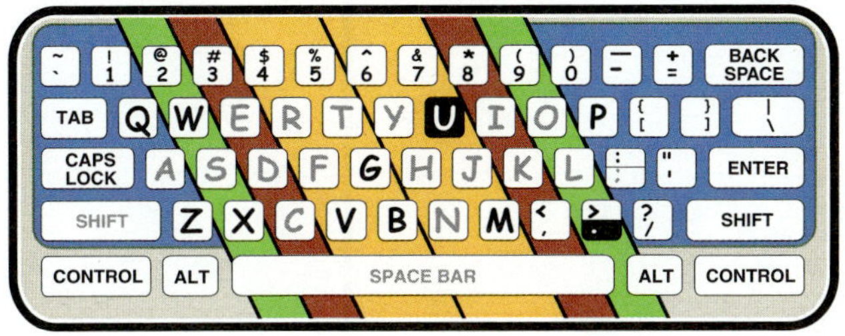

Learn period (.)

1 l . l . l. l. .l. ft. yd. fed.

2 .o. .o. | .h. .h. | .i. .i. | .y. .y. | .;.

3 Jay fell. Jan said. Ken did.

Learn u

4 j u j u ju ju uj uju June June

5 use use; | just just | truck truck

6 out sun jut cut dust hunt rule

Practice period (.) and u

7 You cut it. You unlucky duck.

8 Lucy could dust. You had fun.

9 Ursula is lucky. June ducked.

Bernie's Vocabulary

Do you know what these words mean?

- exquisite
- imagine
- humble

6b Famous Americans

Key the text below in paragraph form.

Walt Disney

Is it possible for a mouse to make you rich? Yes, of course it is. If you do not believe it, look at Walt Disney. Disney came from a humble background. He ended up a rich man. He was a man whose work brought joy to the lives of many.

He brought Mickey Mouse, Donald Duck, and Pluto to life. These are just a few of his exquisite characters. His work continues to be a part of our lives. Families travel miles to step into the amazing world of Disney theme parks. It would be impossible to imagine a world without the works of Walt Disney.

11b Reinforce period (.) and u

Key each line twice; double-space between 2-line groups.

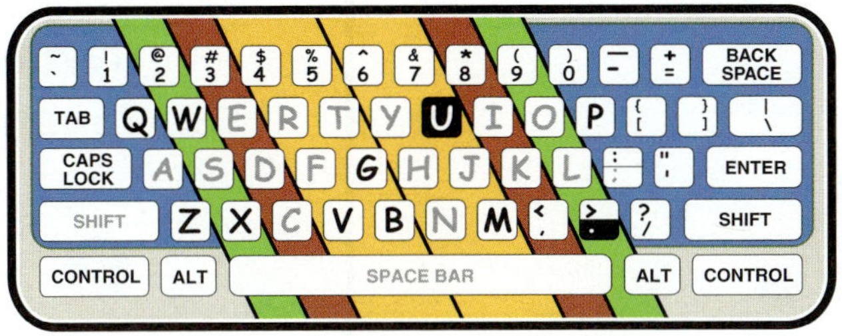

Key letters

1 l. .lc .ly .lh .lr .li .lt .lo
2 ju uh un eu ul uk ur uy tu uju
3 .u U.l J.u eu. Ou. K.u lu. y.u

Key words

4 Okl. Okl. | Ill. Ill. | Ore. Ore.;
5 Utah Utah | rush rush | undo undo;
6 used used | Inc. Inc. | Oct. Oct.;

Key sentences

7 J. Huth just found four cents.
8 Ursula said the candy is sour.
9 Our N. Y. Yankees took second.

Space **once** after a period (.) used with abbreviations and initials.

Skill Builder 6

Bernie's Spelling Words

Key each word four times.

- friends
- January
- Monday
- square
- teacher

6a Balanced-hand Sentences

Key each sentence twice. At the end of each sentence, quickly strike the* Enter *key and immediately begin keying the next sentence. Try to key faster the second time you key the line.

1. It is a big problem for both girls.
2. Keith and I may visit the sorority.
3. The sorority girls kept the big dog.
4. When did they go to the big chapel?
5. Diane and Jane may go to the malls.
6. The maid kept the map of the world.
7. Jake is the big man in right field.
8. Kent may pay Helen to do the forms.

GWAM 1' | 1 | 2 | 3 | 4 | 5 | 6 | 7 |

period (.) and u

candy	**June**
cents	**sick**
eyes	**sour**
fork	**Yankees**
ice	**yes**

11c Speed Building

Key each line twice; double-space between 2-line groups. Strike the Space Bar immediately after keying each word and immediately begin the next word.

1 and and | the the | did did | of of;

2 she she | use use | you you | on on;

3 yes yes | done done | field field;

11d Thinking at the Keyboard

Read the sentences below. From the list at the left, choose the word that best completes the sentence. Key the word and strike the Enter key.

1. Five ________ equal a nickel.
2. Most people like ________ cream cones.
3. When you don't feel well, you are ________.
4. The opposite of no is ________.
5. Jane has blue ________.
6. Most kids like to eat ________.
7. You eat with a ________.
8. The month that follows May is ________.
9. I like the New York Mets and New York _____.
10. A lemon has a ________ taste.

5d Timed Writings

Key two 1' timed writings on each paragraph. Determine your gwam on each timing.

Easy all letters used

• 2 • 4 • 6 • 8 •
You must realize by now that learning to type
10 • 12 • 14 • 16 • 18 •
is fun. But it is not easy. It requires a lot of
20 • 22 • 24 • 26 • 28 •
work. Soon you will quickly be able to type at a
30 • 32 • 34 • 36 •
higher speed than you can print just now.

• 2 • 4 • 6 • 8 •
You should also learn to do neater work using
10 • 12 • 14 • 16 • 18 •
the computer than you do by hand. Quality work at
20 • 22 • 24 • 26 • 28 •
fast rates of speed is the next good goal for you
30 •
to have.

GWAM 1' | 1 | 2 | 3 | 4 | 5 | 6 | 7 | 8 | 9 | 10 |

Lesson 12

p and w

Use a down-and-in thumb motion to strike the **Space Bar**.

12a Learn p and w

Key each line twice; double-space between 2-line groups.

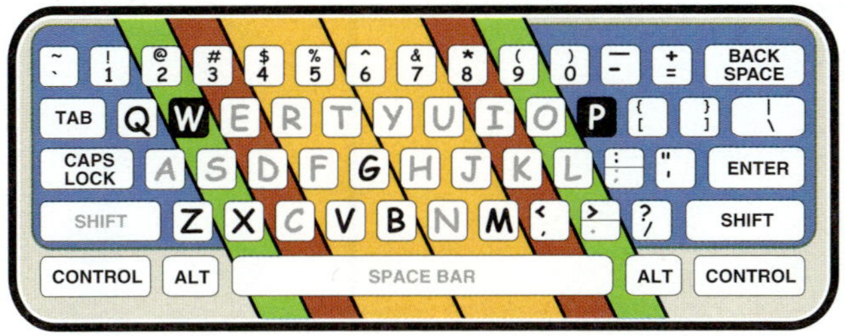

Learn p

1. ; p ; p ;p ;p p;p p;p pup pup;
2. puppy puppy | pop pop | open open;
3. Jo put a pepper on your plate.

Learn w

4. s w s w sw sw ws wsw wash wash
5. was was | away away | awake awake;
6. Lew was to wash away the dust.

Practice p and w

7. paw plow pewter power whip who
8. way pay wait open were prepare
9. Pete was to dust all the pews.

5b Speed Check

Key two 20-second (20") timed writings on each line. Key the line as many times as you can in 20".

| 3 | 6 | 9 | 12 | 15 | 18 | 21 |

1. Jake is skiing.
2. Tamika saw the play.
3. Jorge paved the driveway.
4. Joshua took both of them home.
5. Alonzo is extra quick on the court.

20" | 3 | 6 | 9 | 12 | 15 | 18 | 21 |

5c Where is Bernie?

Key each line twice. As you key the lines, figure out which city Bernie is visiting. Key the name of the city at the end of line 6.

Where is Bernie?

1. There are lots of cable cars in this city.
2. You can see Alcatraz Island from this city.
3. The Golden Gate Bridge is a famous sight here.
4. The most crooked street in the world is here.
5. This city is often called the city by the bay.
6. The name of the city is ____________.

Remember to space twice after a period (.) at the end of a sentence except at line endings. There, press **Enter** without spacing.

12b Reinforce p and w

Key each line twice; double-space between 2-line groups.

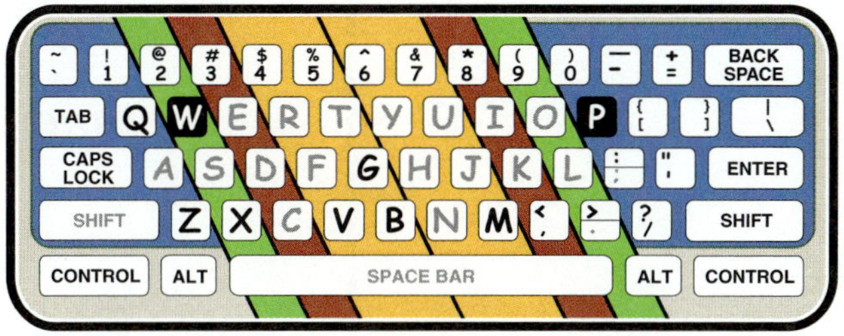

Key letters

1 ;p pu jw aw yp hp kw ew rp opn

2 sw tw .p cp lw dw Jp ip ;w wfw

3 w.u cpy hwI pir otw nep jp wdp

Key words

4 play play | when when | part part;

5 want want | push push | wild wild;

6 path path | pt. pt. | where where;

Key sentences

7 Please do the wash. Jay left.

8 Paul won. I took third place.

9 Petric washed the windowpanes.

Skill Builder 5

Bernie's Spelling Words

Key each word four times.

- above
- dinner
- Saturday
- today
- watch

5a Skill Building

Key each sentence twice. At the end of each sentence, quickly strike the Enter key and immediately begin keying the next sentence. Try to key faster the second time you key the line.

Space bar

1 if of no so as go to do me we be us
2 is do it hi in on ha at see ask let

3 I will eat at the old park at noon.
4 He can go to the game or stay home.
5 Did she try to sell the three hats?

Double Letters

6 feet book leek deep bill moon still
7 green butter kettle school football

8 Kellee said school will start soon.
9 His weekly letters arrived at noon.
10 Jill, Matt, and Bill looked sleepy.

GWAM 1' | 1 | 2 | 3 | 4 | 5 | 6 | 7 |

Check your speed to see how fast you are going.

12c Speed Building

Key each line twice; double-space between 2-line groups.

1. Paul should not take the test.
2. Nicky pitched a perfect ninth.
3. Jane left the flowers for you.
4. Tu will take you to the ranch.
5. Jason left the city yesterday.

12d Speed Check

Key each line once double space. Key a 20-second (20") timed writing on each line. Your rate in gross words a minute (gwam) is shown word-for-word above the lines.

3	6	9	12	15	18

1. I can win.
2. Jay is to stay.
3. Kate threw the rock.
4. I did not start the work.
5. Nick took the car to the lake.

20"	3	6	9	12	15	18

4b Famous Americans

Key the text below in paragraph form.

Susan B. Anthony

Susan B. Anthony made a difference. She worked for the rights of women. She fought to make it possible for women to vote. She felt so strongly about this issue that she signed up and voted in an election. She did this before women had the right to do so.

She also fought for other causes. She was against the use of liquor. She was not in favor of slavery. To voice her views, she organized extra meetings and gave talks. Her dedication to these just causes did not go unrecognized. Her picture is on a dollar coin.

Bernie's Vocabulary

Do you know what these words mean?

- issue
- causes

Lesson 13

Review

13a Short, Easy Words

Key each line twice; double-space between 2-line groups.

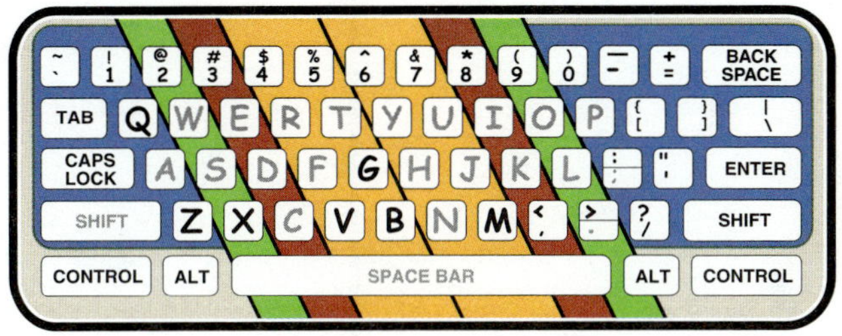

1. was was | push push | enjoy enjoy;
2. into into | deck deck | loaf loaf;
3. Joan Joan | lost lost | drop drop;
4. fake fake | rush rush | sick sick;
5. away away | earth earth | joy joy;
6. Jeff Jeff | kind kind | pay pay;
7. juice juice | wash wash | ill ill;
8. drink drink | rice rice | key key;

Skill Builder 4

Bernie's Spelling Words

Key each word four times.

- important
- printer
- secret
- stopped
- treasurer

4a Balanced-hand Sentences

Key each sentence twice. At the end of each sentence, quickly strike the Enter key and immediately begin keying the next sentence. Try to key faster the second time you key the line.

1. Duane may go with them to the city.
2. Their box of forms is by the chair.
3. Ruth may work with the eight girls.
4. The dog is by the big field of hay.
5. Did they own the title to the land?
6. Pamela may pay for the eight signs.
7. I may go to the city to visit them.
8. The men kept busy with their audit.

GWAM 1' | 1 | 2 | 3 | 4 | 5 | 6 | 7 |

Quickly strike the **Space Bar** after the last letter in each word. Immediately begin keying the next word.

13b Sentences

Key each line twice; double-space between 2-line groups.

1. Jess is to help with the work.
2. I can see the nurse in a week.
3. You should take the class now.
4. Kaye will take a trip to Iowa.
5. Jo is to work with us all day.
6. Kayla and Nancy just found us.
7. Jan said the roof was too low.
8. Hector just left for the lake.

Check to see whether your typing speed on a 1' timed writing has increased.

3d Timed Writings

Key two 1′ timed writings on each paragraph. Determine your gwam on each timing.

Easy all letters used

• 2 • 4 • 6 • 8 •
Keep in home position all of the fingers not
10 • 12 • 14 • 16 • 18 •
being used to strike a key. Do not let the fingers
20 • 22 • 24 • 26 • 28 •
move out of position for the next letters in your
30
copy.

• 2 • 4 • 6 • 8
You have control over your fingers. Seize
• 10 • 12 • 14 • 16 • 18
that control. See how quickly speed goes up when
• 20 • 22 • 24 • 26 • 28
you learn that you can make them do just what you
• 30 • 32
expect them to do.

GWAM 1' | 1 | 2 | 3 | 4 | 5 | 6 | 7 | 8 | 9 | 10 |

13c Technique: Enter Key

Key each line twice. At the end of each line, strike the Enter key and immediately begin keying the next line.

1 I can see.
2 Joe said no.
3 Kit has a car.
4 Kellee has left.
5 Kay was the first.
6 Ohka had three hits.
7 Juan saw the ice show.
8 Judith saw the two deer.

13d Something Extra

Unscramble the letters below to create ten words. Key those words.

sjtu	eekw	leph	wken	dsia
sihw	lypa	desu	ofdnu	enrsu

3b Speed Check

Key two 20-second (20") timed writings on each line. Key the line as many times as you can in 20". Your rate in gross words a minute (gwam) is shown below the lines.

| 3 | 6 | 9 | 12 | 15 | 18 | 21 |

1. Kate called me.
2. Jorge was the champ.
3. Lance wanted a Zorro mask.
4. Did you buy Paul a basketball?
5. I have an extra ticket for Enrique.

20" | 3 | 6 | 9 | 12 | 15 | 18 | 21 |

3c Where is Bernie?

Key each line twice. As you key the lines, figure out which city Bernie is visiting. Key the name of the city at the end of line 6.

1. There are lots of beaches.
2. You can visit movie studios in this city.
3. The Hollywood Bowl features great music.
4. You can see Mickey Mouse at Disneyland .
5. The Dodgers and the Lakers play in this city.
6. The name of the city is ___________.

Where is Bernie?

Lesson 14

m and g

14a Learn m and g

Key each line twice; double-space between 2-line groups.

Learn m

1 j m j m jm jm mjm mjm man man;

2 may may | major major | camp camp;

3 mop man sum come moon must Pam

Learn g

4 f g f g fg fg gf gfg eggs eggs

5 golf golf | leg leg | eagle eagle;

6 Ingrid Higgins can go golfing.

Practice m and g

7 gym mug gum game muggy gimmick

8 jam gain mail eight gram kings

9 giggled moments juggled memory

Skill Builder 3

Let's review the keys for letters S through Z.

Bernie's Spelling Words

Key each word four times.

- access
- across
- bridge
- together
- window

3a Letter Review

Key each line twice; double-space between 2-line groups.

s 1 Stan sold us his six season passes.

t 2 Trent went to Seattle to see Brent.

u 3 That music museum is quite unusual.

v 4 Eva had over seventy vivid violets.

w 5 Will knew we had two weeks of work.

x 6 Rex Xiong explained the excise tax.

y 7 Joy and I may buy the keys in July.

z 8 Liz told Zane about the lazy zebra.

GWAM 1' | 1 | 2 | 3 | 4 | 5 | 6 | 7 |

Are your fingers curved and upright, or are you getting sloppy? If you are sloppy, you won't be able to reach the highest keying speeds.

14b Reinforce m and g

Key each line twice; double-space between 2-line groups.

Key letters

1 jm pm mw .m ym mc Mh rm im mtm
2 fg og ng fh eg gk gj dg fg g.g
3 mg mpg wgm gmu ;m. gcy mhr gim

Key words

4 glum glum | milk milk | eggs eggs;
5 mug mug | make make | groom groom;
6 gum gum | music music | gate gate;

Key sentences

7 Mary took three games to play.
8 Megan got groceries on Monday.
9 Mel and Logan had good grades.

Learn to Key a Report Title Page

1. Use 1-inch or default side margins.
2. Set the alignment to *center*.
3. Begin keying 2 inches from the top of the page.
4. Press the **Caps Lock** key. Key the title of the report in all capital letters. Press the **Caps Lock** key again to turn off all capitals.
5. Key "Prepared by:" and your name about 5 inches from the top of the page.
6. Key the current date about 8 inches from the top of the page.

2d Report Title Page

Key the text below as a short report.

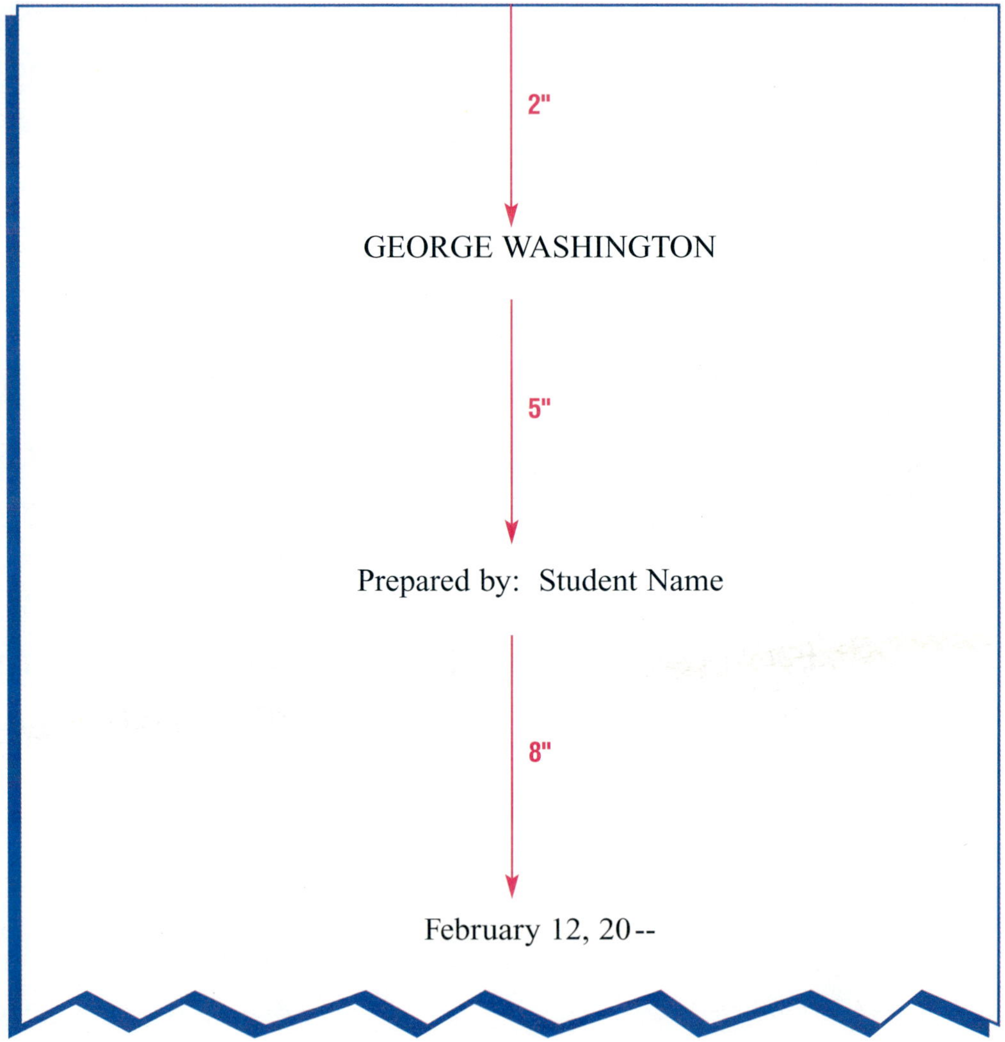

m and g

awake	**moon**
earth	**nurse**
golf	**point**
gym	**roof**
low	**wild**

14c Speed Building

Key each line twice; double-space between 2-line groups. Strike the* Space Bar *immediately after keying each word and immediately begin the next word.

1 add add | cut cut | due due | or or;
2 for for | got got | not not | so so;
3 told told | with with | year year;

14d Thinking at the Keyboard

Read the sentences below. From the list at the left, choose the word that best completes the sentence. Key the word and strike the* Enter *key.

1 If you are not asleep, you are ________.
2 If a horse is not tame, it is ________.
3 Pt. stands for pint or ________.
4 Another name for soil is ________.
5 The top of a house is the ________.
6 The opposite of high is ________.
7 A ________ works in a hospital.
8 A game where you hit a ball is ________.
9 You see the ________ in the sky at night.
10 You play basketball in a ________.

Learn to Key a Short Report

1. Set the line spacing to *two* or *double*.
2. Use 1-inch or default side margins.
3. Begin keying 2 inches from the top of the page.
4. Press the **Caps Lock** key. Key the title of the report (GEORGE WASHINGTON) in all capital letters. Press the **Caps Lock** key again to turn off all capitals.
5. Use the alignment feature of your software to center the title.
6. Strike the **Tab** key to indent the paragraphs.
7. Strike the **Enter** key only at the end of the paragraphs.

2c Short Report

Key the text below as a short report.

2"

GEORGE WASHINGTON

I was born in Virginia. I grew up on a farm. As a young boy, I enjoyed math. I was also excited by the great outdoors. Being a surveyor was a natural job for me with my liking of math and the outdoors.

Later in life I became quite interested in serving my country. I fought in the American Revolution. I helped defeat the British. This was an amazing time in our history. Later I became the first President of our great country. My name is George Washington.

Lesson 15

right shift and b

Learn to Key Capital Letters

Use these three steps to key capital letters with the left hand:

1. Hold down the **Right Shift** key with the little finger on the right hand.
2. Strike the letter with the left hand.
3. Return your finger(s) to the home keys.

15a Learn right shift and b

Key each line twice; double-space between 2-line groups.

Learn right shift

1 ; F ; F ; E ; E ; C ; C ; S ;S

2 Ruth Ruth | Stan Stan | Anne Anne;

3 Rob Cey; Jake Smith; Dick Falk

Learn b

4 f b f b fb fb bf bfb base base

5 bus bus | bug bug | bubble bubble;

6 Brook brought back a baseball.

Practice right shift and b

7 Bob and Bill can buy the book.

8 Beth Barber borrowed the ball.

9 Ben Babbitt obeyed both signs.

Learn to Key Paragraphs

1. Use the alignment feature of your software to center the title (George Washington).
2. Set the line spacing to *two* or *double*.
3. Strike the **Tab** key to indent the paragraphs.
4. Strike the **Enter** key only at the end of the paragraphs.

Bernie's Vocabulary

Do you know what these words or terms mean?

- surveyor
- American Revolution

2b Famous Americans

Key the text below in paragraph form.

George Washington

I was born in Virginia. I grew up on a farm. As a young boy, I enjoyed math. I was also excited by the great outdoors. Being a surveyor was a natural job for me with my liking of math and the outdoors.

Later in life I became quite interested in serving my country. I fought in the American Revolution. I helped defeat the British. This was an amazing time in our history. Later I became the first President of our great country. My name is George Washington.

15b Reinforce right shift and b

Key each line twice; double-space between 2-line groups.

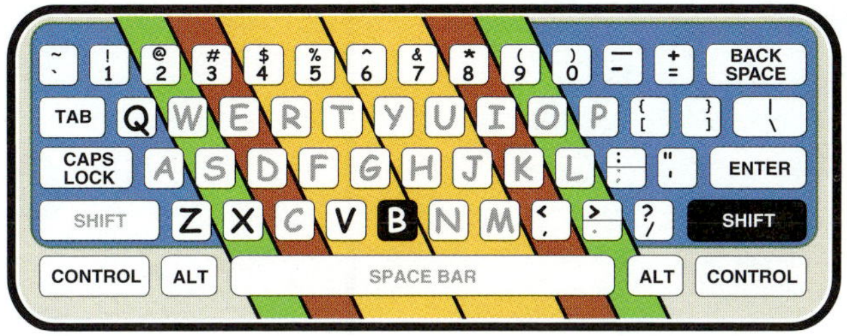

Key letters

1. gG pF ;W pE ;D pT ;C Ap S; R;R
2. fb mb gb bw jp ub yb kc hb rbi
3. lb ;yC ubi Dpo mTn T;W EpR SpA

Key words

4. blue blue | oboe oboe | both both;
5. Russ Russ | Rob Rob | Bobby Bobby;
6. boy boy | brake brake | able able;

Key sentences

7. I bought a baseball for Bruce.
8. Brent will buy the buns today.
9. Ray and Brenda won both games.

Make sure you key the word faster the second time you key it in lines 4–6.

Skill Builder 2

Bernie's Spelling Words

Key each word four times.

- asked
- May
- often
- quite
- water

2a Letter Review

Key each line twice; double-space between 2-line groups.

j	1	Jess, Joy, and Jane just saw Jerry.
k	2	Jo kept her knickers in a knapsack.
l	3	Bill left the will with the lawyer.
m	4	I sent the minimum amount of money.
n	5	Nan left at noon on the nineteenth.
o	6	Don and Tom took two books to read.
p	7	Paul asked Pat to pass the peppers.
q	8	I included equal, equip, and quite.
r	9	Roberto arrived after Richard left.

GWAM 1' | 1 | 2 | 3 | 4 | 5 | 6 | 7 |

right shift and b

15c Speed Check

Key each line once double space. Key a 20-second (20") timed writing on each line. Your rate in gross words a minute (gwam) is shown word-for-word above the lines.

3 | 6 | 9 | 12 | 15 | 18

1. I took it.
2. Meg did not go.
3. Maria got a new job.
4. I left my bike at school.
5. Bo said the surf was too high.

20" | 3 | 6 | 9 | 12 | 15 | 18

15d Where is Bernie?

Key each line once. As you key the lines, figure out which city Bernie is visiting. Key the name of the city at the end of line 6.

1. The Yankees play in this city.
2. This city is also known as the Big Apple.
3. The United Nations is located here.
4. Broadway plays take place in this city.
5. Wall Street is in this city.
6. The name of the city is ___________.

Learn to Key Timed Writings

Set the line spacing to *two* or *double*. Use the **Tab** key to indent the paragraphs. Strike the **Enter** key only at the end of a paragraph. At the end of a full line, the text and insertion point move to the next line automatically. This is called **word wrap**.

The dots and numbers above the words show the number of words per minute you key. The dots are for the odd numbers. The first dot is for 1; the second dot is for 3.

1d Timed Writings

Key two 1' timed writings on each paragraph. Determine your gwam on each timing.

Easy all letters used

• 2 • 4 • 6 • 8 •
Are you one of the people who often look from
10 • 12 • 14 • 16 • 18 • 20
the copy to the screen and down at your hands? If you
• 22 • 24 • 26 • 28 • 30 •
are, you can be sure that you will not build a speed to
32 • 34 • 36 • 38 •
prize. Make eyes on copy your next goal.

• 2 • 4 • 6 • 8 •
When you move the eyes from the copy to check
10 • 12 • 14 • 16 • 18 •
the screen, you may lose your place and waste time
20 • 22 • 24 • 26 • 28 •
trying to find it. Lost time can lower your speed
30 • 32 • 34 • 36 • 38 •
quickly and in a major way, so do not look away.

GWAM 1' | 1 | 2 | 3 | 4 | 5 | 6 | 7 | 8 | 9 | 10 |

Lesson 16

Review

16a Words

Key each line twice; double-space between 2-line groups.

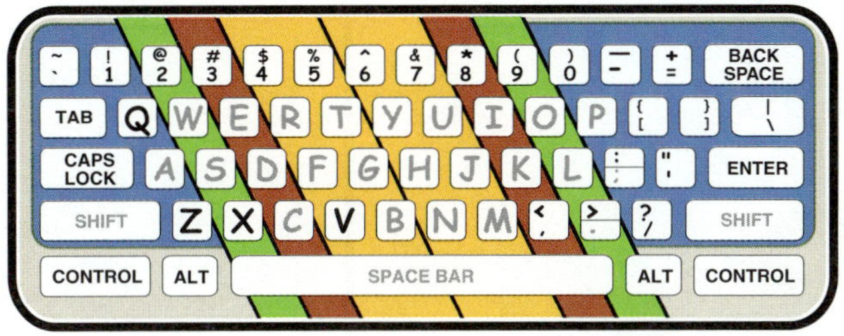

1. boat boat | game game | wasp wasp;
2. hike hike | leaf leaf | yard yard;
3. judge judge | cent cent | boy boy;
4. Miguel Miguel | oboe oboe | no no;
5. change change | top top | was was;
6. felt felt | read read | yoke yoke;
7. Justin Justin | Ken Ken | Ann Ann;
8. Jerry Jerry | Meg Meg | Gary Gary;

1b Speed Check

Key two 20-second (20") timed writings on each line. Key the line as many times as you can in 20". Your rate in gross words a minute (gwam) is shown below the lines.

3 | 6 | 9 | 12 | 15 | 18 | 21

1. Jake has a dog.
2. Tim missed the quiz.
3. Nick brought the flowers.
4. Polly, when is your next exam?
5. Every girl voted for Jose Lopez.

20" | 3 | 6 | 9 | 12 | 15 | 18 | 21

Where is Bernie?

1c Where is Bernie?

Key each line twice. As you key the lines, figure out which city Bernie is visiting. Key the name of the city at the end of line 6.

1. The Liberty Bell can be seen here.
2. Independence Hall is located in this city.
3. The Continental Congress met in this city.
4. Benjamin Franklin lived here for many years.
5. This city was the first capital of the U.S.A.
6. The name of the city is ___________.

16b Sentences

Key each line twice; double-space between 2-line groups.

1. Roy may be able to do the job.
2. Gregg should be on time today.
3. K. C. Cane was here on Friday.
4. The park may open this Sunday.
5. Seth left early; Chase stayed.
6. Omar and Maria were both here.
7. Jerry used our last free pass.
8. Karl and Jan went to the game.

Remember to strike **Enter** without spacing after a period at the end of a line.

Skill Builder 1

Let's review the keys for letters A through I.

Bernie's Spelling Words

Key each word four times.

- very
- away
- show
- were
- park

1a Letter Review

Key each line twice; double-space between 2-line groups.

a 1 Anna Adams ate an apple and banana.

b 2 Bobby Cubbage bobbled the baseball.

c 3 Chuck checked on the cute raccoons.

d 4 Don decided to hide the old fiddle.

e 5 He believes it may rise three feet.

f 6 I shot fifty free throws on Friday.

g 7 Gregg, Glenda, and Gus were guests.

h 8 Here is the other half of the hymn.

i 9 I picked Illinois, Idaho, and Iowa.

GWAM 1' | 1 | 2 | 3 | 4 | 5 | 6 | 7 |

16c Balanced-hand Sentences

Key each sentence twice. At the end of each sentence, quickly strike the* Enter *key and immediately begin keying the next sentence.

1. He is to go.
2. I kept a sign.
3. She may sign it.
4. They own the land.
5. Pay the maid for it.
6. Kay paid for the sign.
7. Helen owns all the land.
8. Jan and I work with gusto.

16d Something Extra

Unscramble the letters below to create ten words. Key those words.

apkr	eehr	emga	tobh	eonp
aydr	iftg	hpta	deubg	alemt

Unit 2 Skill Building

Objectives

In this unit you will:

- Review the alphabetic keys
- Type words, sentences, and paragraphs
- Use correct keying techniques
- Think at the keyboard
- Compose at the keyboard
- Learn to spell words
- Learn about famous Americans
- Learn new vocabulary words
- Increase your keyboarding skill

Lesson 17

v and comma (,)

Reach down to the comma and v keys without moving your hands toward your body.

17a Learn v and comma (,)

Key each line twice; double-space between 2-line groups.

Learn v

1. f v f v fv fv vfv vfv van van;
2. vase vase | vague vague | van van;
3. every even; very; seven vivid;

Learn comma (,)

4. k , k , k, k, ,k ,k ,k, ,k, ,k
5. Ann, Jose, Mike, Maria, Julio,
6. Buy milk, tea, eggs, and corn.

Practice v and comma (,)

7. Vicky, Evan, and Val said yes.
8. Eva spelled vivid and victory.
9. Even Elva visited the volcano.

22c Balanced-hand Sentences

Key each sentence twice. At the end of each sentence, quickly strike the* Enter *key and immediately begin keying the next sentence.

1. tab → He paid the man.
2. tab → Lana may visit us.
3. tab → The girl may pay us.
4. tab → Dick may fix the sign.
5. tab → Kris bid on the antique.
6. tab → He may do the work for us.
7. tab → They may focus on the audit.
8. tab → The six signs are by the dock.

22d Something Extra

Unscramble the letters below to create ten words. Key those words.

zqiu	rebv	mhat	gesg	wkla
ianp	ujts	aftc	aoytd	aerxt

17b Reinforce v and comma (,)

Key each line twice; double-space between 2-line groups.

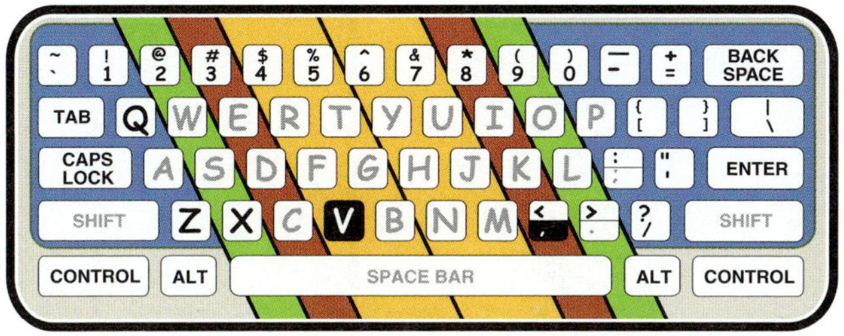

Key letters

1 fv Vb vm ,g ,p ,w uv cv yv vJv
2 ,h ,I ,r vo vT vn e, k, d, ,C,
3 av lv, ;vs vfv ,k, Jv, vEi ,Wv

Key words

4 vote vote | ever ever | even even;
5 Joan, Joan | Rick, Rick | Eve, Eve
6 five five | save save | dove, dove

Key sentences

7 Evan, Ken, and I got new hats.
8 Bev, Steve, and Ron were late.
9 Kevin voted for J. R. Ventura.

Reach up to the third-row keys without moving your hands away from your body.

22b Sentences

Key each line twice; double-space between 2-line groups.

1. Ticha went to the art exhibit.
2. Carlos quit the job on Monday.
3. Frank gave the quiz to LaToya.
4. Judy put the paper on my desk.
5. Florida plays next on Tuesday.
6. The quiz took over four hours.
7. Jose wants to go to Green Bay.
8. The art museum opens tomorrow.

v and comma (,)

baseball	**Friday**
bases	**oboe**
brake	**job**
bubble	**volcano**
even	**vote**

17c Speed Building

*Key each line twice; double-space between 2-line groups. Strike the **Space Bar** immediately after keying each word and immediately begin the next word.*

1. up up | sign sign | sure sure | I I;
2. go go | put put | file file | of of;
3. set set | hour hour | along along

17d Thinking at the Keyboard

Key the sentences below. From the list at the left, choose the word that best completes the sentence.

1. A little round ball is called a ________.
2. You blow a ________.
3. You run around the ________.
4. To stop a car, you step on the ________.
5. An ________ is a musical instrument.
6. You get a ________ to earn money.
7. Saturday comes after ________.
8. Molten or hot rock comes out of a ________.
9. You ________ in an election.
10. If the score is tied, it is ________.

Lesson 22

Review

Reduce the amount of time between keying words. Quickly strike the **Space Bar** after you finish a word and immediately begin keying the next word.

22a Short, Easy Words

Key each line twice; double-space between 2-line groups.

1 quit quit | maze maze | back back;

2 every every | got got | exam, exam

3 Josh Josh | fawn fawn | paid paid?

4 old old | equal equal | vase vase:

5 six six | candy candy | haze, haze

6 few few | milk milk | budge budge;

7 Rick Rick | joke joke | dart dart?

8 pet pet | hymn hymn | drive drive:

Lesson 18

x and colon (:)

Leave 2 spaces after a colon (:) within a sentence.

18a Learn x and colon (:)

Key each line twice; double-space between 2-line groups.

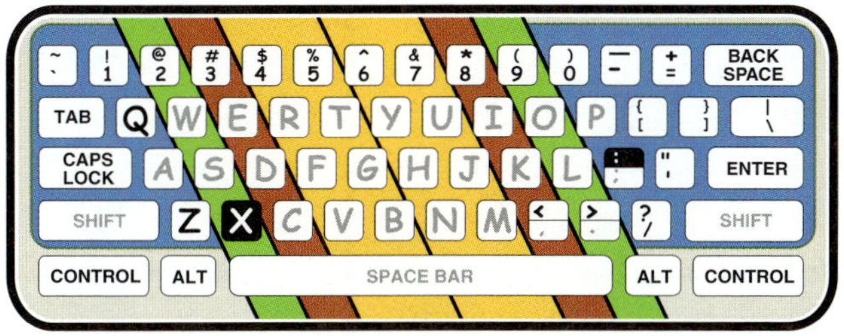

Learn x

1 s x s x sx sx xsx xsx six six;

2 six six | exit exit | exert exert;

3 Max put sixteen exit signs up.

Learn colon (:)

4 ; : ; : ;: ;: :; :; :a: :l: :l

5 To: Ship To: From: Bill To:

6 Note: Date: Dear Dr. Baxter:

Practice x and colon (:)

7 Three won: Rex, Max, and Tex.

8 New Keys: B and X | To: M. Pax

9 Reply To: Maxine Xiong | Dates:

Where is Bernie?

21c Speed Check

Key each line once double space. Key a 20-second (20") timed writing on each line. Your rate in gross words a minute (gwam) is shown word-for-word above the lines.

3	6	9	12	15	18

1. I can see.
2. Jo went skiing.
3. Tim caught the ball.
4. Zelda may quit next week.
5. Two of the five boys finished.

20"	3	6	9	12	15	18

21d Where is Bernie?

Key each line once. As you key the lines, figure out which city Bernie is visiting. Key the name of the city at the end of line 6.

1. The city is located on the Great Lakes.
2. It is the third most populated city in the U.S.
3. You can visit the Sears Tower here.
4. Wrigley Field is a landmark in this city.
5. The city was once almost destroyed by fire.
6. The name of the city is ___________.

18b Reinforce x and colon (:)

Key each line twice; double-space between 2-line groups.

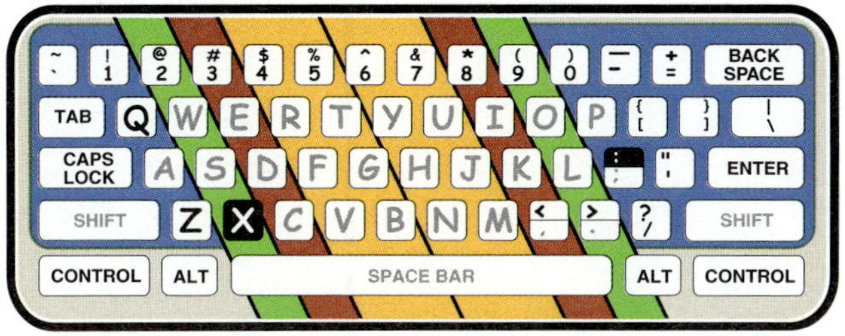

Key letters

1 sx ,x vx ;: b: m: g: xp wp xK:
2 :u :c :y x. xh XJ i: r: o: x:x
3 xte axn dxl s:f j:e :n. c: ,y:

Key words

4 six six | extra extra | exam exam:
5 box box | exact exact | exit exit:
6 Dear Mr. Cey: Dear Dr. Cedeno

Key sentences

7 Dick expects us to explain it.
8 He included fox, box, and tax.
9 To: Juan Mota | From: Karl Cox

Key steadily through each line without pausing.

21b Reinforce z and tab

Key each line twice; double-space between 2-line groups.

Key letters

1 az qz z? xz :z vz ,z zB mz gzp

2 wz. Zuc yzh zir otz nzj zK; zu

3 ezj azk fzl szd zq? X:z v,z bz

Key words

4 Zack tab → Jay tab → Dan tab → Zelda

5 Zoro tab → Ray tab → Ken tab → Zeke

6 Zoro tab → zinc tab → zip tab → zebra

Key sentences

7 Zack Martinez went to the zoo.

8 Zo was amazed by the lazy pup.

9 Liza was puzzled by the speed.

18c Speed Check

Key each line once double space. Key a 20-second (20") timed writing on each line. Your rate in gross words a minute (gwam) is shown word-for-word above the lines.

1. Jo may go.
2. Lexie can work.
3. I even hit a triple.
4. The game took four hours.
5. Jan likes to play video games.

20" | 3 | 6 | 9 | 12 | 15 | 18 |

18d Where is Bernie?

Key each line once. As you key the lines, figure out which city Bernie is visiting. Key the name of the city at the end of line 6.

1. Paul Revere lived here.
2. This city is a state capital.
3. The JFK Library is located here.
4. A famous tea party took place here.
5. Bunker Hill is a famous landmark here.
6. The name of the city is ____________.

Lesson 21

z and tab key

The **Tab** key is used to leave space between columns and to indent the first line of a paragraph.

21a Learn z and tab key

Key each line twice; double-space between 2-line groups.

Learn z

1. a z a z az az za za zero zero:
2. zoo zoo | zero zero | dizzy, dizzy
3. real cozy; too lazy; to zigzag

Learn tab key

4. Jack tab → Ben tab → Kay tab → Maria
5. one tab → two tab → three tab → four
6. five tab → six tab → seven tab → eight

Practice z and tab key

7. tab → Zelda said Zach was lazy.
8. tab → Zo took the zoology quiz.
9. tab → Liza Zeman is at the zoo.

Lesson 19

Review

Reach up to third-row keys without moving your hands away from you. Reach down to first-row keys without moving your hands toward you.

19a Short, Easy Words

Key each line twice; double-space between 2-line groups.

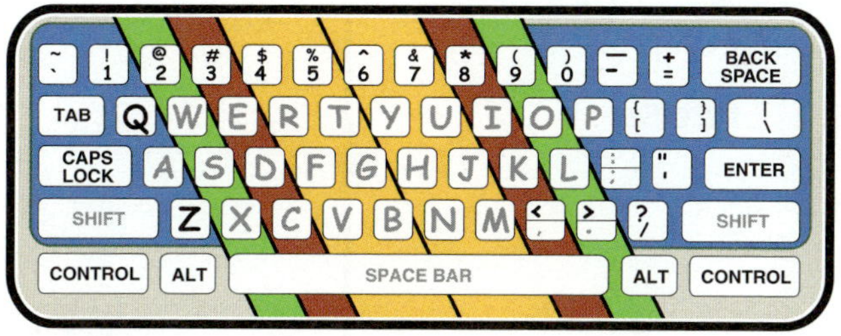

1 view view | extra extra | bay, bay

2 glob glob | mop mop | jerky jerky;

3 fen fen | desk desk | catch catch:

4 Javy Javy | Dave Dave | Mary Mary:

5 inch inch | dent dent | save save;

6 the the | nice nice | until, until

7 six six | have have | candy candy;

8 bog bog | fake fake | power power:

basket	**quarts**
box	**quit**
chair	**six**
exam	**tax**
fake	**true**

20c Speed Building

Key each line twice; double-space between 2-line groups. Strike the Space Bar immediately after keying each word and immediately begin the next word.

1 fit fit | bank bank | of of | do do:
2 form form | give give | each, each
3 more more | into into | city city

20d Thinking at the Keyboard

Key the sentences below. From the list at the left, choose the word that best completes the sentence.

1. One more than five is ________.
2. You pack things in a ________.
3. Another name for a test is an ________.
4. You pay ________ on most things you buy.
5. The opposite of real is ________.
6. You shoot a ball at a ________.
7. You sit on a ________.
8. When you stop, you ________.
9. Four ________ equal a gallon.
10. The opposite of false is ________.

19b Sentences

Key each line twice; double-space between 2-line groups.

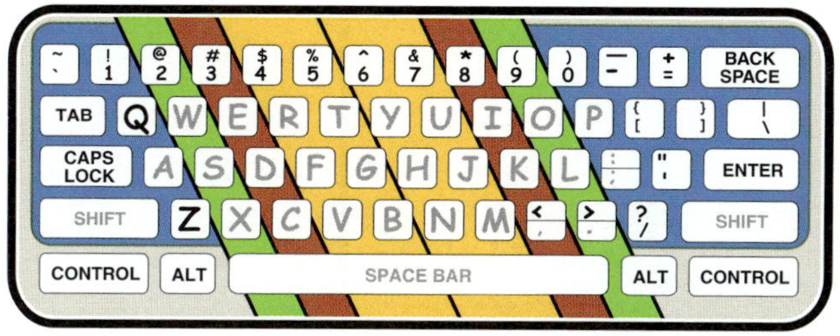

1. Rex took the bus trip to Utah.
2. Dave may manage the new store.
3. Jack found the key last night.
4. Jorge rode a bike to the lake.
5. Nakia watched all of the game.
6. Jo played seven extra innings.
7. Chandra made the final basket.
8. Gavin expects us to win today.

20b Reinforce q and question mark (?)

Key each line twice; double-space between 2-line groups.

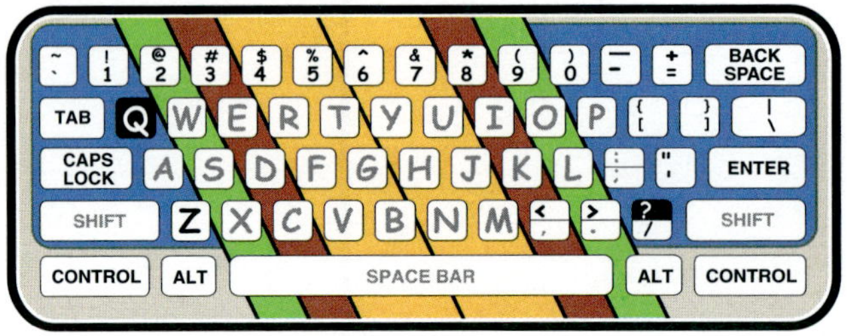

Key letters

1 aq xq :q ;? V? b? q, qm qg qCy

2 ?h ?i ?r qY eq qn ?u ?p ?w jqk

3 qdl kqa sQm fQ? M?n xQ? Q? Jqy

Key words

4 six six | extra extra | exam exam:

5 box box | exact exact | exit exit:

6 When? Why? What? How? Who?

Key sentences

7 When did Raquel quit the team?

8 Why did he question the squad?

9 How quickly did Quint qualify?

Leave two spaces after a question mark (?) at the end of a sentence except at line endings. There, strike **Enter** without spacing.

19c Balanced-hand Sentences

Key each sentence twice. At the end of each sentence, quickly strike the Enter key and immediately begin keying the next sentence.

1. He may fix it.
2. Kay may keep it.
3. Glen held the dog.
4. Jan works with them.
5. They may keep the fox.
6. The man is by the cycle.
7. The chair is in the field.
8. Helen is by the turn signal.

19d Something Extra

Unscramble the letters below to create ten words. Key those words.

leph	vfei	txie	cabk	armg
kowr	uspc	kipc	eidly	jnyoe

Lesson 20

q and question mark (?)

20a Learn q and question mark (?)

Key each line twice; double-space between 2-line groups.

Learn q

1 a q a q aq aq qa qa quit quit;

2 aqua aqua | quad quad | quip quip;

3 square equal quart quote equip

Learn question mark (?)

4 ; ? ; ? ;? ;? ?; ?; Why? When?

5 What? Who is it? Is it true?

6 Did she call? What day is it?

Practice q and question mark (?)

7 Require it? He quit? She is?

8 He questioned Raquel and Quin.

9 How many quarts? Did he quit?